Modular Approaches
to the Study of the Mind

MODULAR
APPROACHES
TO THE STUDY OF THE MIND

NOAM CHOMSKY

First Distinguished Graduate Research Lecture
San Diego State University

San Diego State University Press

Noam Chomsky
Modular Approaches to the Study of the Mind
San Diego, California
San Diego State University Press
p. xi, 114

Hardback ISBN   0-916304-56-6
Paperback ISBN   0-916304-55-8

Library of Congress Cataloging in Publication Data

Chomsky, Noam
Title
Bibliography
Index

1. Linguistics   2. Cognitive Psychology   3. Title   4. Chomsky, bibliography

Library of Congress No. 82-62962

Designed by Rachael Bernier

CONTENTS

The Distinguished Graduate Research Lecture Series

The Distinguished Graduate Research Lecture Series of San Diego State University brings eminent scientists and scholars of national and international status to the campus to present "all-University" graduate colloquia on generic problems of research and graduate education. These colloquia combine open lectures of general interest with smaller seminars and workshops for the graduate students and faculty who are actively pursuing research in areas related to the colloquia topics. The series is sponsored by the Graduate Division and Research and the University Research Council, and is supported in part through Instructionally Related Activities Funds. Each academic discipline or department which offers a graduate degree at San Diego State University may nominate notable scholars to participate in the series. Exposure to and interaction with such distinguished researchers is an integral part of the instructional experience for all graduate students at San Diego State University. Each of the lectures in the series will be published to assure their increased availability to the students and faculty of the University, and to the community at large. This book, *Modular Approaches to the Study of the Mind* by Noam Chomsky, originated as the First San Diego State University Distinguished Graduate Research Lecture.

Noam Chomsky: A Biographical Sketch

Noam Chomsky was born on December 7, 1928 in Philadephia, Pennsylvania. His undergraduate and graduate years were spent at the University of Pennsylvania, where he received his Ph.D. in linguistics in 1955. During the years 1951 to 1955, while a Junior Fellow of the Harvard University Society of Fellows, he completed his doctoral dissertation, entitled "Transformational Analysis." The major theoretical viewpoints of the dissertation appeared in the monograph *Syntactic Structures,* which was published in 1957. This formed part of a more extensive work, *The Logical Structure of Linguistic Theory,* which circulated in mimeograph in 1955 and was published in 1975.

Chomsky joined the staff of the Massachusetts Institute of Technology in 1955 and in 1961 was appointed full professor in the Department of Modern Languages and Linguistics (now the Department of Linguistics and Philosophy) and in the Research Laboratory of Electronics. He was appointed in 1966 to the Ferrari P. Ward Professorship of Modern Languages and Linguistics, and in 1976 he was appointed Institute Professor.

Professor Chomsky has extended his teaching and research outside his home campus on many occasions. In 1958-1959 he was in residence at the Institute for Advanced Study at Princeton, New Jersey; in 1962 he was Research Fellow in Cognitive Studies at the Center for Cognitive Studies at Harvard University, in the summer of 1966 he served as Linguistic Society of America Professor at the Linguistic Institute at the University of California, Los Angeles, and during the fall and winter terms of 1966-1967 he was Visiting Beckman Professor of English at the University of California, Berkeley. In the spring of 1969 Chomsky delivered the John Locke Lectures at Oxford and the Shearman Lectures at University College, London; in January of 1970 he delivered the Bertrand Russell Memorial Lectures at Cambridge University, London. In 1972 he delivered the Nehru Memorial Lectures in New Delhi, and in 1977 the Huizinga Lecture in Leiden, among many others in the United States and abroad.

Chomsky has received honorary degrees at the University of London, University of Chicago, Loyola University of Chicago, Swarthmore College, Delhi University, Bard College, and the University of Massachusetts. He is a Fellow of the American Academy of Arts and Sciences and a member of the National Academy of Science, as well as other national and international professional and learned societies. He is the author of numerous books and articles on linguistics, philosophy, intellectual history and contemporary issues, and his works have been the subject of much analysis by other scholars and commentators. A comprehensive bibliography of works by and about Noam Chomsky appears at the end of this book.

1

Modular Approaches to the Study of the Mind

I would like to sketch out a range of problems that fall within what is sometimes called cognitive psychology, a field which attempts to approach questions of human thought in the spirit of rational inquiry, putting aside and dismissing dogmatic methodological constraints such as those typical of the several varieties of behaviorism that flourished some years ago. As I will be using the term, cognitive psychology incorporates parts of a number of disciplines—philosophy, psychology, linguistics, artificial intelligence—and anticipates the forging of closer links with the neural sciences and general biology.

It has proven quite profitable to approach the problems of cognitive psychology as problems within a theory of mental representations and computations on these representations. I would like to discuss a number of questions that arise in connection with this conception and a number of problems that can be submitted to inquiry if we adopt it. The scope of these remarks will be fairly broad, and correspondingly the treatment of particular questions will necessarily be somewhat superficial. On some of these topics, there is further—sometimes substantial— literature. This is particularly true in the theory of vision, visual perception, imagery, in some aspects of the theory of language, and perhaps in a few other areas. The perspective that I will adopt here is in part historical: that is, I will attempt to explain how these problems were viewed, formulated and understood at the dawn of what we might regard as cognitive psychology in the modern sense several hundred years ago. Secondly, I will discuss how these problems are viewed today. In some few of these areas, there have been real advances; in many others, there has been a notable lack of progress. This disparity may itself be revealing with regard to the nature of human intelligence viewed as a specific biological system with particular limits and particular character and incorporating specific modes of inquiry and understanding that may simply not be appropriately adapted and designed for the study of certain questions. This view is commonly regarded as unintelligible, but it seems to me very plausible.

Plainly, the first question that comes to mind about mental representations is what they are, or maybe whether they are anything. That is essentially the problem of dualism: What are we talking about when we talk about the mind as distinct from the body? A secondary aspect of this question, assuming that we can convince ourselves that it makes sense to talk about mental representations at all, is that of the circumstances under which it is appropriate to postulate them. For example, it is commonly argued that it makes sense to postulate mental representations in, say, the study of language and understanding of language, or in interpretation of visual space, but it is not appropriate to postulate them in the study of how one knows how to ride a bicycle.

Assuming these questions to receive some kind of an answer, we convince ourselves that it is appropriate in some circumstances to postulate and talk about mental representations. The second major question is that of the nature of mental representations. What are they? What are their properties? Here we can divide the inquiry into a number of sub-questions. First is what is sometimes called the format problem, what you might call "the syntax of mental representations." Of what elements are they composed and how are they put together? The second aspect of this is what you might call the system problem. That is, how are various cognitive systems—systems of knowledge and belief— organized and interrelated? Here the question of modularity arises. Is the organization of cognitive structures uniform and homogeneous across domains, or are there separate systems, what you might think of metaphorically as "mental organs" on the analogy to organs of the body? The latter viewpoint, which I think is correct, is what John Marshall has called "the new organology,"* referring to Franz Josef Gall, whose work he argues—I think rather plausibly—has been much understood and underrated.

A third aspect of the problem of the nature of mental representations is what we might call the rule problem. That is, the question of whether—assuming that there are mental organs in this sense—there are cognitive structures with their own particular properties and structures; the question of whether in some cases it might be appropriate to charaterize these structures in terms of a system of rules that determines their properties. Language is a case in point. We might ask whether the concept of grammar is in some extended sense of this term appropriate in the case of other mental organs as well.

If we settle somehow the question about the nature of mental representations, the third class of problems has to do with the relation of these "mental organs" to other aspects of the world. Here there are again a number of sub-questions.

* A reference list for scholars mentioned in the text will be found at the end of Chapter 2, pp. 51-52.

The first question is how mental representations enter into thought and action—what is sometimes called their "causal role," to use a common but I think rather misleading phrase. To be concrete, suppose I believe that it will rain and therefore take my coat to work. My belief that it will rain would be thought of in these terms as a mental representation which somehow encodes this belief in what Jerry Fodor has called "the language of thought." We can ask how this relation between me and the belief enters into my action, in particular, say, my act of taking my raincoat. Or, we can ask how my knowledge of English enters into what I am doing right now, speaking certain things. Or how does my knowledge of the properties of three-dimensional space enter my interpretation of what I see?

A second and perhaps deeper question is that having to do with the origins of these systems of belief and knowledge. How do mental organs develop in our minds? How do we acquire our knowledge of particular things, of language, or arithmetic, or the structure of personality, or the system of social structures in which we live, or the behavior of objects in three-dimensional space and so on? A final question related to this is that of consciousness and acessibility. That is, to what extent are we aware, and can we in principle become aware, of the mental representations which are postulated in their earlier steps to function and to relate somehow to what we do, to our action?

I think it is fair to say that virtually all of these questions were placed on the modern intellectual agenda by Descartes about 350 years ago, and in many respects we are still wrestling with his questions. I think his version of them deserves some attention. This is plainly the case with regard to the first of these questions, that of the ontological status, the existence of mental representation. The traditional, classical approach to these questions—the Cartesian approach—is in fact familiar. You recall that Descartes postulated two substances, the body and mind, which are separate, and that a major question arises as to how they are related, and so on. One tends these days to disparage this approach, but it is worth bearing in mind that Descartes had reasons, many of which are worth considering. In fact, many of these reasons for the Cartesian dualism arise in a rather embarrassing form today, I think, and therefore are worth serious consideration.

How did Descartes actually arrive at this dualistic picture, or how can we reconstruct the way that he arrived at it? He did what was reasonable; he began with the concept of body. He had some concept of mechanics, and his concept of body was what we might call from our mechanics one which involved bodies pushing each other and bumping into each other and pulling each other and so on. In terms of this conception of contact mechanics, Descartes thought that he could explain everything in the world of inanimate objects and everything having to do with animals, and a good deal that had to do with humans. But he demonstrated that there was a limit, that there was a residue beyond the reach of mechanics in the sense in which he defined the notion. This residue involves a number of things, but one element that entered into it crucially was the matter of choice and will.

Let me now quote from an expositer of Descartes at the time, La Forge. The residue involves what he calls "that secret disposition of the invisible parts of the body of the animal, and principally of its brain, according to which, after being imprinted by an object, man feels incited and inclined—and the animal fels compelled—to make appropriate actions and movements." There is in short a distinction between man and machine—a chasm between man and machine—man being incited and inclined and machines being impelled to act in a certain fashion under the pressure of external contingencies.

Why is man only incited and inclined? The reason, continuing with La Forge's exposition, is that "the soul, despite the disposition of the body, can prevent these movements when it has the ability to reflect on its actions and when the body is able to obey." For example the Cartesians argued, surely correctly, that we can choose to cause ourselves harm if we want, which indicates that though we are incited and inclined to avoid pain, we could choose to run into the fire, and so on. We can choose this deliberately. In the course of this exposition, Descartes stressed a number of interesting examples having to do with the use of language. He pointed out that the characteristic use of language is unbounded; it has not particular limits. We can say anything, in other words. He argued also that the use of language is free from stimulus control. Furthermore, Descartes said that the use of language is somehow appropriate to situations and evokes in other minds the thought we have in our mind. These three characteristics, the characteristics of being unbounded, free from stimulus control and evocative and/or appropriate, we might call "the creative aspect of language use." It is quite true that these are characteristics of the normal everyday use of language. Decartes offered this as one striking example of the ability of the soul to choose in a way in which a machine cannot. How does the soul choose? Well, not by mechanical principles, where again we recall what he meant by mechanics. A parrot or a machine could in fact produce language-like things, but not with this creative aspect, Descartes argued. Therefore, he felt that some new principle was required—we might call it a "creative principle"—which goes beyond the mechanical principle characteristic of bodies. Within his substance metaphysics this second principle became a second substance, namely, mind, of which the essence is thought: a thinking substance.

How does it work? How does the soul choose, given that it follows this creative principle? The Cartesian view was that this is a mystery, in fact an impenetrable mystery. Descartes argued that we may not "have intelligence enough" to comprehend how free action can be indeterminate, though "we are so conscious of the liberty and indifference which exists in us, that there is nothing we comprehend more clearly and perfectly." And "it would be absurd to doubt that of which we

6

inwardly experience and perceive as existing within ourselves, just because we do not comprehend a matter which from its nature we know to be incomprehensible."

He is saying that the ability to choose, the fact that we are only incited and inclined, not compelled, is phenomenologically obvious. That is, our ability to choose is as clear to us as the fact that we see the color red when we look at something red, and so on. That part seems quite plausible. He also said that we know this phenomenologically obvious property to be incomprehensible. Here one can perhaps question the conclusion in certain respects. One may ask whether we know or only surmise that the nature of this matter is incomprehensible and we might also ask whether it is incomprehensible in principle to undifferentiated mind as Descartes argued, where mind is not a property of the biological world at all. These conclusions can be questioned; I will come back to them. Nevertheless, it seems to me that one cannot lightly disregard the point that he was making. That is, surely no one has proposed a reasonable answer to these questions as of today. And it is quite possible that if there is an answer, it lies beyond human intelligence, which from our point of view it makes sense to think of as just a specific biological system.

If you look at physics, or the history of ideas, or the theory of evolution or whatever, it seems to me that no reason has been advanced to lead us to suppose that we can find answers to the questions we can pose except in certain very narrow domains. It could turn out that questions of this sort lie beyond the bounds of the specific biological system which is human intelligence. That is a speculation, but it might not be an implausible one. Descartes, remember, postulated a creative principle which belongs to mind in addition to the mechanical principle which characterizes body. The theory quickly collapsed in subsequent years, but it is interesting to note how it collapsed. What collapsed was not the theory of mind but rather the theory of body. That is, Newton demonstrated a few years later that bodies do not behave in the manner of Cartesian automata. They do not follow the principles of Cartesian mechanics. Therefore, Newton postulated what from his point of view and the point view of the time was a mysterious force, a property of bodies which violated the principle of Cartesian mechanics, namely the principle of action at a distance. If you look at the seventeenth and eighteenth century debate over physics, you find that many continental physicists rejected Newtonian mechanics because of its appeal to this occult principle of action at a distance, something which is plainly inconceivable.

Now, the logic of Newton's successful postulation of action at a distance is rather similar to Descartes's postulation of a creative principle. That is, in each case what was argued was that given principles, say the principles of Cartesian mechanics, could not extend to a certain domain. Newton showed convincingly that they could not extend to the explanation of the motion of the heavenly bodies and therefore postulated a new principle, an occult principle, to account for this. Descartes argued that they could not extend to the questions of will and choice, and therefore he postulated another occult principle, namely the creative principle. Of course there is a difference, namely that Newton made his principle do some work; that is, it really had explanatory force. It is just barely conceivable that Descartes did too. In fact, he destroyed his work on the mind when he heard what had happened to Galileo, so we don't know exactly what he succeeded in doing, although it is reasonable to suppose that it did not reach very far. In any event, there is a challenge to develop a theory of mind and to show that it will do some work, a challenge which has not been met too magnificiently in the 350 years that have passed since.

Where does the Cartesian argument stand after the theory of bodies has collapsed? We conclude that bodies are not Cartesian mechanisms. But as far as Descartes's problems are concerned, we have no further insight into them. They stand where they were. The crucial moral to draw from this story, I think, is the following: If one wants to treat the mind-body problem as a problem of reducibility, a problem of reducing talk about mind to talk about bodies, then we have to do what Descartes did. We have to start with a concept of body, with some notion of body. But, as this historical exercise shows, the fact of the matter is that we really have no concept of body: the concept of body is open and evolving. It changes. It changes with new discoveries. In fact, the concept of body simply includes whatever is moderately well understood. In Descartes's time, it included push-pull mechanics. A generation after Newton, when action at a distance had become part of scientific common sense, it included that. Later, it included electromagnetic forces, and who knows what it will include tomorrow? The moral, then, is just to try to understand more, taking whatever we come to understand to some degree, taking that to be a property of what we will call body. The further moral is that we really should not worry very much about the onotological status of what we postulate, expecting the progressive assimilation of parts of cognitive psychology to the natural sciences as matters progress. So I do not really think that the ontological question, the question of the existence of mental representations, is ultimately a very serious problem, because the presupposition that we start with some closed concept of body is not satisfied and has never been satisfied. That is one of the lessons of the scientific revolution of the last several hundred years.

Let us turn to the second question: Under what circumstances is it appropriate to postulate mental representations? Here the Cartesian answer apparently was that we should always do so; that is, that thinking always enters into every aspect of human action and behavior. But here it seems to me useful to depart from the Cartesian framework and make some distinctions. We can pose the following empirical question: Is it correct to appeal to internal mental representations and computations, or is it not? This is a question of fact. The answer can be yes or no depending on whether this gives an accurate or an inaccurate characterization of the way the mind works. To illustrate what is at stake, we can think of a question that does not have to do with human behavior at all. Somehow those are easier to think about. Suppose we have the problem of designing a missile which will hit the moon. Let us imagine two different ways of doing this. One missile uses the principle that was proposed by B.F. Skinner, I guess during the Second World War, which probably would work in theory. The idea is to have a bunch of pigeons in the nose cone with some kind of picture of the moon focused on a screen, and have the pigeons trained so that when the missile veers off course, the right pigeon pecks, which does something to cause the missile to veer back on course—a kind of servomechanism. That missile in principle should hit the moon.

Now let us imagine another missile which operates differently. It has built into it the laws of physics and information about the bodies in the solar system, about the moon, the sun, their distances, etc. Also, it has information about its initial position and velocity. The missile carries out calculations comparing its position with the projection of the position of the moon and adjusting its course in terms of these computations.

These two missiles might do exactly the same thing. They might manifest the very same behavior. But they would in fact be functioning quite differently. For the first one it would be improper, incorrect, to postulate the analog of a system of mental representations. On the other hand, for the second one it would be correct. It would in fact be correct to say that it has something analogous to mental representations, that it has internal representations and is using computations on these representations.

As this hypothetical example illustrates, it might be impossible to determine just by observing the behavior of the system which of the two kinds it is. We would have to do more sophisticated things like taking it apart or subjecting it to some further tests, but still there could be a right or wrong answer, right in one case, wrong in the other. The same is true when we turn to the harder questions, the questions, say, of the use of language and so on. It is a question of fact whether the system is working one way or the other way.

It is fairly commonly argued that the system of language is like the missile with the pigeons. Michael Dummett, an Oxford philosopher, suggests that knowledge is a practical ability. It is the ability to do certain things, the ability to speak, to understand, to determine whether sentences are well-formed, and so on. That view has a certain superficial plausibility; certainly, it is widely repeated. However, I think the plausibility disappears when we begin to inquire a little more carefully into the nature of this ability; that is, when we ask ourselves why we have the ability to determine, say, that a certain sentence has a certain meaning instead of some other meaning when this is a sentence we have never heard—the normal situation.

Let me give you a couple of concrete examples just to have something on which to hang the rest of the discussion. Take the following sentence: "John is too clever to expect us to catch Bill." Ask yourself who is doing the expecting. Well, the answer is John. that is, what it means is that John is so clever that he, John, doesn't expect us to catch Bill.

Now consider the virtually identical sentence, "John is too clever to expect us to catch." Who is doing the expecting? Well, if you think about that, what it means is that John is so clever that someone, not John, doesn't expect us to catch John. John is so clever that one shouldn't expect us to catch him. Now if you compare those two sentences, which differ just in the presence of "Bill," notice that you make a different decision; that is, the computing system in your mind makes a different decision about what is the unexpressed subject of the verb "expect." It is a pretty subtle calculation if you think about it, and it doesn't come about because it is the only interpretation that makes sense. The others would all make perfect sense, but there is something about the system of the mind that forces that conclusion on you.

Take another case. Take the sentence, "John bought Mary a dog to play with." Ask yourself who is playing with whom. What it means is that Mary is playing with the dog. That is, John bought Mary a dog for Mary to play with the dog. Well, of course that again is unexpressed. That is, it is a contribution of your mind. One might ask why your mind does not draw some other conclusion. Why doesn't the sentence mean that John bought Mary a dog for Mary to play with John, let's say. Or, that John bought Mary a dog for the dog to play with John. Or, that John bought Mary a dog for the dog to play with Mary. Again, the judgment that you make is an extremely subtle one, and it is not represented in the form of the sentence. Nor is it selected on the basis of what would be a plausible meaning, because any of those interpretations would be plausible. In fact, the subtlety is really quite astonishing in this case. Recall the sentence again: "John bought Mary a dog to play with," meaning for Mary to play with the dog, not for the dog to play with Mary. In fact, try to imagine the difference of meaning between Mary playing with the dog and the dog playing with Mary. If there is a difference of meaning at all, it is a very subtle one. Mary is playing with the dog if and only if the dog is playing with Mary. "Play with" is a symmetrical predicate in this case. Therefore, any facts that determine that Mary is playing with the dog also determine that the dog is playing with Mary. So it is extremely hard to see, if you were trying to make up a training sequence about these sentences, how you could even distinguish their meanings. Nevertheless, we all know that "John bought Mary a dog to play with" means for Mary to play with the dog. That is, we unerringly select one of two near-synonymous expressions as the paraphrase.

Similarly, we reject all the others, which are also quite plausible.

These are quite typical examples. Incidentally, these are pretty simple sentences. They are eight or ten words long, much below the average sentence length, and involve much less computation than is necessary in our normal use of language, in listening and reading, and so on. Nevertheless, they immediately illustrate, as soon as you begin to take them seriously, that quite precise and rather subtle judgments are made uniformly and instantaneously, and of course unconsciously, as we come to terms with phrases, as we somehow break them into their parts and perform an analysis of them, as our minds do. These examples are quite characteristic. I pick them only because there is some understanding of what the reason is in this case. There are many other cases where there is no understanding. It is all very well to say that our knowledge of language is a practical ability to do so and so, but as soon as we begin to take the facts seriously, as soon as we try, in other words, to characterize that ability, then we are quickly compelled to attribute to the mind a system of rules, a system of principles of some kind that somehow computes representations of linguistic expressions in highly specific ways. For example, in the case that I gave, our minds compute a representation which identifies the subject of "expect," differently in the two cases depending on whether "Bill" was present or not, and what is the subject of "play with," and so on. I say that we are *compelled* to conclude that there is a system of rules that generates representations of this kind. Of course we are not compelled logically to do so; it is just that no other approach has ever been proposed. In fact, every approach that goes beyond hand-waving postulates a system of rules of that kind, what we might call a grammar.

There is a good deal of discussion and debate in the philosophical, psychological and linquistic literature about the legitimacy of this move towards postulation of grammar, but I really think that there is nothing to discuss unless some coherent alternative is proposed. A serious look at the nature of the problem makes one rather disinclined to put much credence in the likelihood of such an alternative. We are in this sense compelled to postulate grammars.

So much for the first question. Let us turn to the second—the nature of systems of mental representations. Here is where the real work is. Here is where there has been real progress, and correspondingly here is where I am not going to say anything. To go into this question would require giving a course, not a talk, because there is something really to talk about. In the case of language, there has been some real progress in the last couple of years in developing principles that will explain facts of the kind that I just described. In this particular case, there is good reason to believe that the principles involve binding of variables, and are in a sense somewhat like those of logic, but not quite because the binding principles are really language-specific rather than a priori logical principles. I will give the name "binding principles" to the principles that in fact determine the results that I just described, and I will then say that these binding principles are somehow represented in your mind.

In the case of vision, there are similar things to say. There are now interesting theories of visual processing that account for fact that could be regarded as somewhat comparable to the linguistic examples that I mentioned. For example, it seems to be a fact that if you are shown successive presentations in space, you will interpret them as the motion of a rigid body. Now that does not have to be true. Or, for example, suppose I were to present to you a plane figure at, say, 90 degrees to the line of sight, and then rotate it until it looked like a line, parallel to the line of sight. What you would perceive is just what I described, a plane figure rotating, though in fact there is another obvious interpretation, namely, that it could be a plane figure shrinking until it disappears. Nevertheless, what you perceive is a plane figure rotating. Similarly, a certain sequence of presentations will be interpreted by the eye as a cube in motion, and so on.

Both of these things appear to reflect a certain principle—let us call it a "rigidity principle"—which is essentially this: The mind, the visual system, works on the assumption that what you are seeing is a rigid object in motion. Now that does not have to be true, and it could be false, but that seems to be the way the mind processes visual information over a large range. We might think of this rigidity principle, which has been reasonably well studied, as being analogous to the binding principles which yield the linguistic facts I mentioned.

One crucial area of inquiry is to determine these systems in various domains. Although to proceed very far into these topics would go well beyond the scope of these remarks, it is here that the question of modularity arises. The traditional view of modularity, the Cartesian view, is that there is no modularity. Descartes's view is that "there is within us but one soul, and this soul has not in itself any diversity of parts. . . . The mind is entirely indivisible." In short, there are no mechanisms of mind. This view shows up elsewhere and has in fact quite a long tradition. It appears in a modern version in psychology, for example. In a spectrum of opinion that ranges from Skinner at the one extreme to Piaget at the other (which includes just about everyone) this homogeneity principle is adopted. Piaget does assume a kind of cognitive modularity; that there are stages of cognitive development. However, crucially in the Piagetian and Geneva theories, at each stage of cognitive development the principles that have been attained are uniform across all domains. They are not differentiated from system to system. It follows, and Piaget and his associates conclude that, for example, the structures of language are reflections of earlier structures in other domains. The structures of language are, they claim, reflections of sensori-motor constructions. In fact, quite generally in experimental and cognitive and developmental psychology, and also in philosophy and other areas, artificial intelligence for example, it has been a dominant motif. It is assumed that the mind is homogeneous, that there are principles, inductive principles, analytic principles, problem-solving mechanisms, that are applied simply in one domain or another, but always the same principles.

We can ask—again, a question of fact—we can ask if that is true. For example, take the rigidity principle in vision and the binding principles in language. Are they in fact reducible to the same principle? Do they belong to the same system of principles? That is a question of fact. We do not have time to go into it, but the examples may suggest that the principles are entirely distinct. It is hard even to think of some vague analog in one domain for the principles that seem applicable in the other domain. These examples are a little misleading because I have presented the principles atomistically. When you show how they fit into an integrated system of principles, I think the conclusion becomes even more obvious. It simply seems to be the case that the systems that we begin to understand, at least, are quite separate. Of course they interact; vision and language undoubtedly interact in all sorts of ways. We talk about what we see, and so on. But the principles that determine the properties of these systems seem quite diffeent; they seem to develop in different ways and they have different properties, and there seems to be no useful analogy among them in the various systems. It is an empirical matter, so of course there is room for doubt, but it seems to me that the facts lead us to the conclusion that the structure of mind is in fact modular, which shouldn't be terribly surprising despite the common assumption to the contrary. Every complex biological system we know is highly modular in its internal structure. It should not be a terrible surprise to discover that the human mind is just like other complex biological systems: that it is composed of interacting sub-systems with their specific properties and character and with specific modes of interaction among the various parts.

I should say that when we look at a particular system, say language, we also find internal modularity. That is, we find sub-systems with their own quite specific properties interacting in highly determined ways. In fact, it seems to me fair to say that wherever we know anything, that is what we discover. It could be that in the vast areas where we do not know anything it is different, but that seems a rather dubious conclusion. It seems to me that the assumption of modularity, of the "new organology," is really rather well supported, at least in the areas where we know something.

Let us turn to the third class of questions, namely the relation of mental organs to other aspects of the world. Remember, the first question to be asked here is how our mental representations play what is called their "causal role" in determining what we do. Here, the classical Cartesian view is that there is nothing to say. Now here one has to be little cautious. Remember, the Cartesian view is that, not being machines, we are incited and inclined, but not compelled, to do certain things. Notice that that leaves open some possibilities. For example, the possibility that there might be a very good predictive theory of behavior. We might be able to predict, say, that if I were to train a machine gun on a crowd and tell them to repeat after me some slogan, then everybody would do it. We might be able to predict that with a high degree of accuracy. Nevertheless, it is still a crucial fact that each person could choose to do otherwise. So the possibility of constructing a predictive theory is a long way away from getting a real explanation of what is involved in choosing, even if what you choose is predictable statistically, or maybe even 100 percent for all we know.

In other words, there is a fundamental difference between a theory, maybe even a successful theory, of prediction of human behavior or of motivation on the one hand, and a real explanation of interminate action on the other. There is a crucial distinction between being compelled and being inclined, maybe highly inclined, and as far as that crucial issue is concerned, it seems to me that modern cognitive psychology, or modern thought in general, has nothing much to contribute. I don't think it has any proposal to make as to what may be involved in this. So that question, which is a rather central one, seems to remain exactly in the mysterious state in which it was in the earliest speculations (and recall that it was at the core of Descartes's dualist argument). It is in this sense that I think that argument has to be taken quite seriously, though not its specific conclusions.

Let us turn to a topic where there is a little more hope, at least a little more progress, namely the second question: How do the mental representations relate to experience? That is another question about the relation between mental representations and the world; the question of the origins of beliefs and knowledge.

Here, the Cartesian theory is rather interesting and worth some careful thought. Descartes asks us to imagine an infant who has had no revelant visual experience, and who looks at a figure drawn on paper, a figure of a triangle, and who sees a triangle. Descartes asks what is really going on in this case. What the infant actually sees, of course, is not a geometrical triangle. Rather, what it sees is a somewhat irregular figure with the corners not quite coming together and the bottom line a litle bit curved and so on. At least that is the retinal image, but it is true that what you would perceive, or so Descartes claims, probably correctly, is a distorted triangle. You would see the thing to be a distorted triangle, not a perfect example but some crazy figure. The question he asks is why that is true. Why would the infant without experience perceive a distorted triangle rather than a perfect example of some plane figure? Descartes's answer is that the mind is essentially organized in terms of the principles of Euclidian geometry. Therefore, the mind imposes an exemplar, a kind of model, and it interprets what it sees in terms of this exemplar.

The argument that Descartes presents is an important one. It is sometimes called an argument from poverty of the stimulus. It is not that we learn that the things we see are distorted triangles (in fact, Descartes imagines the case of an infant who has had no relevant experience); rather, this is what the mind does in the absence of any experience. That is a classical argument; it goes back to Plato, and it is a good argument. If we find that the mind is doing something in the absence of relevant experience, we have to attribute what it is doing to the intrinsic structure of the mind. Similarly, in studying, say, the growth of the body, if we discover that the liver develops in the way it does in the absence of sufficient directive information in the immediate environment, say the nutritional environment, to determine the course of development, then everyone assumes without further thought that it is an intrinsic process of maturation and growth, internally directed, that is determining that this collection of cells becomes the liver, and so on. It is a good argument, it is a classical one, and it is one that can be incorporated into modern analysis of these questions as well, and should be. In fact, take the cases I mentioned—the case of the binding principle and the rigidity principle. In these cases, it is quite plausible—in fact, if you think about it is overwhelmingly obvious—that these principles are vastly underdetermined by the evidence available. It is particularly clear in the language case because you just do not have any relevant evidence at all. It is pretty clear that these principles are simply part of the system by which we attain knowledge, rather than being something that we learn through experience. I do not really see how any other conclusion is possible if we pay attention to the facts. Again, it seems particularly clear in the case of language, where expressions that are entirely new to us are nevertheless given quite precise interpretations in accordance with very reasonable principles, principles that are not a priori true, but nevertheless are very reasonable and have quite an explanatory range.

That is the general line of thinking that has been most productive, and I think it a very reasonable one. Of course, it is non-demonstrative, these being empirical subjects, not mathematics but I think it is rather persuasive when you look at the details. Let us assume that it is and think a little bit further about these questions of origins of knowledge and belief.

The vast bulk of the discussion in epistemology and in psychology is atomistic in a certain sense; that is, one asks questions like how do I know or why do I believe that all ravens are black, or that if it is cloudy it will rain, and so on. You take particular items of knowledge and belief and ask how they arise as items of knowledge or belief. The analogy in the case I have mentioned would be: How do you know or why do you believe that such and such a sentence means such and such, or that such and such a series of presentations is a cube in motion, let's say. The answer in these cases, it appears, is non-atomistic. That is, you know this or you believe this because a certain system of knowledge simply grows in the mind, yielding as a consequence particular items of knowledge, for which there is no inductive basis and in fact no grounding in experience. The principles that determine this knowledge—say the principles of binding of variables and rigidity—appear to be innate principles of the mind, what you might call biological a priori principles. Now notice that a mind does not have to be organized in these ways; it is not a matter of logical necessity. You could design a mind that operated differently. However, it seems to be true that the mind is in fact organized in these ways.

A number of conclusions might be drawn. The first is that if the mind lacked these principles—as it might, since they are not logically necessary—we would have no relevant experience, hence no learning. This is a familiar Kantian point. There is a more complex variant of it which is perhaps more interesting: If the mind had different principles, it might have the very same experience but nevertheless different knowledge. For example, suppose some Martian had the same sensory system that we have but did not have the rigidity principle and the binding principle. Given exactly the data we have been presented with, the Martian might develop a different set of beliefs; in the case of language, a different system of knowledge. Whereas we know that expression such and such means so and so, the Martian would know just as well that that expression means some different thing; and whereas we perceive that the object is rotating, the Martian would perceive it as shrinking. That is, different systems of knowledge and belief could arise on the basis of exactly the same experience if the mind were simply organized in terms of different principles.

This observation bears on the concept of knowledge. Now, the traditional approach to knowledge is to think of it roughly as follows: Knowledge is true belief which is grounded in experience in some fashion, and people are supposed to have reasons for what they know. It is well known that there are problems in this view. There are standard problems which show that justification is not a strong enough requirement, that you need something even stronger. However, the examples I have been discussing seem to cut the other way. They show that you may have knowledge with no justification at all. Take for example our knowledge that this expression means such and such, or that this object is a cube in motion, or that an object moving along a parabola will emerge from behind a screen at a given point. All these cases of knowledge could be cases for which there is no warrant or grounding or justification at all. They are simply cases of knowledge that are consequences of systems of principles rooted in the mind, and which lead to the growth of cognitive structures in a certain direction. If that is right, then the traditional picture is wrong in essence. It is just not the way knowledge is organized; it is the wrong way of thinking about the question of knowledge. Hence, the tradition really has to be recast. The questions have to be rethought in some different fashion.

The traditional picture may be right in certain domains. For example, it may be correct to say, just as a matter of fact, that our knowledge that all ravens are black is based on inductive evidence, but that is just a question of fact. We could imagine a different mind with different principles for which that was a piece of knowledge that developed as a consequence of biological a priori principles. In other words, nothing involving justification is conceptually essential to the notion of knowledge. Rather, it is a question of fact which pieces of knowledge are of one type and which are of other types.

For areas that are important to human life, knowledge claims must be grounded; for example, in science, in the laborious construction of systems of knowledge. However, over a very substantial domain of human knowledge, and which is really in a sense at the core of our existence and function, it seems that this is the wrong picture and that our knowledge develops in quite different ways. In short, the traditional approach to knowledge seems dubious and perhaps wrong. In many interesting cases it seems that systems of knowledge simply grow and mature in the mind, leading to particular cases of knowledge over quite large, in fact infinite domains.

This carries us to what you might call the ontogenetic problem: How do all these systems develop? Where the conventional approach seems reasonable, say with regard to the fact that all ravens are black, it makes sense to look for inductive evidence and grounding and all the traditional concepts of epistemology. However, in the case of the examples that I gave from vision or language, where the growth of knowledge seems somehow organic rather than atomistic, this seems like the wrong approach altogether. The whole process seems more like maturation, like the growth of an organ. In other words, we are led back to a kind of organology, to the idea that mental organs develop in the way physical organs do, perhaps under the triggering effect of experience but along an internally directed course. There could very well be learning around the periphery. Again, in areas that are crucial for human life, that seems to be true in fact. In this area, knowledge claims have to be grounded, but for a large core of human knowledge and experience it seems that knowledge claims and beliefs are not grounded but nevertheless may be valid.

A final comment about the last point, accessibility to consciousness: Can we gain access to our mental representations? Again, a long tradition says we can. It is at the heart of the Cartesian approach. It is crucial to the rationalist approach that if you really think hard you can gain access to the clear and distinct ideas which lie at the core of your perception and knowledge, and so on. Those are accessible to the mind in principle. It is obviously true in the case of the empiricists, at least the ones who are clearest about what they said; for example, David Hume, for whom the mind is just like a theater in which the ideas are the players. They appear on the stage, and the mind is just this appearance of ideas on the stage before the mind's eye. Plainly, they are accessible. It also seems to be true in the philosophy of Kant, who writes that ". . . all representations have a necessary relation to a *possible* empirical consciousness. For if they did not have this, and if it were altogether impossible to become conscious of them, this would practically amount to the admission of their non-existence." This seems to be a very strong and explicit claim about the accessibility of mental representations, and I think if you trace the ideas up to the modern period that is pretty common. In fact, even in the case of Freud, with all the emphasis on the unconscious, if you really look at what he wrote, there are textual questions. Most Freud scholars would probably disagree with what I am now going to say, but I think that it is true. It seems to me if you look at the text carefully, you find that when Freud talks about inaccessibility, as he sometimes does, the context indicates that this is a kind of loose talk, and what he really means is difficulty of access.

In the modern discussion it has often been held to be more

or less criterial for the existence of mental representations that you should be able to perceive that in fact they are there. This discussion has come up in the context of the notion of following rules, of rule-guided behavior. It has often been argued that if you want to claim that someone is actually following rules, you have to be able to show that, when it is brought to his attention, the person can tell you that those are the rules he is following. Plainly, that is not the case in any of the examples I have discussed. For example, in the case of what I referred to as the binding principles, there is absolutely no way for you to think hard and conclude finally, "Oh, yes, that's what I'm doing." If those are the only principles you are following, the only way we can find that out is by treating ourselves from the outside, trying to construct theories about ourselves, much as we construct theories about, say, the nature of the sun. We have no internal access to it, no introspective access. The same is true in many of these cases: the growth of arms, the growth and use of the rigidity principle, and of the binding principles. If somebody comes up with an alternative, we can then take a look at that proposal and see if it is plausible. However, as long as no proposal is made, there is nothing to say.

2

COLLOQUIUM:
RESEARCH IN LINGUISTICS

The material in this chapter is extracted from the comments and responses by Professor Chomsky at the research colloquium which followed his formal lecture at San Diego State University, November 17, 1980.

Chomsky

I will just make a few remarks and then throw the thing open to discussion so we have a colloquium instead of another speech. Perhaps I ought to make a few comments about the kind of work that I and others have been engaged in for the past twenty-five years or so, and try to give some assessment about where it is now.

There was, I think, one major conceptual change that took place at the origins of the work in what is now called generative grammar, and that really didn't lead to inconsistencies with other theories but to concern with a new type of question. To put it at its simplest, I think the change was a change of focus from the study of language to the study of grammar.

In the whole long and very rich history of what is now called linguistics, the object of investigation was essentially language; that is, people wanted to find what the elements were of particular languages, where the properties of those elements were, and so on. The grammar was just the set of statements the linguist put together that characterized that entity called a language.

Generative grammar has a totally different concern. From the point of view of generative grammar, language may not even exist. In fact, in my view it is very unclear what the notion of language refers to, if anything. Language is not one of the things in the real world; that is, it isn't a thing out there. Whatever it is, it's some sort of complex derived notion, maybe no notion: In fact, it doesn't seem to be a linguistic notion, at least not linguistically definable. However, there is something in the real world, namely, what's in your head and what's in my head, more or less shared between your head and my head, that makes this discussion possible. That is something in the real world, but it is not a language—we don't have a language in our heads. Rather, what we have in our heads is some kind of system of rules that determines the properties of expressions over an indefinite range.

That system of rules is what is called grammar. The term is misleading because it is very different from the kind of grammar that a traditional grammarian wrote. It may overlap in some respects but its purpose is different; therefore, it will tend to develop in a different way. The grammar in our head is something in the real world. In fact, the grammar is part of the characterization of the present state of an organism. It is as much a part of the real world as your system of visual processing is part of the real world. There is something about your visual cortex that makes you different from an insect and makes you like other mammals. Whatever that is, it is real, and the grammar that you have in your heads is essentially on a par with that.

As the shift of focus goes from language to grammar, a new domain of investigation opens. Maybe linguistics is a misleading term for this new discipline, which really belongs to the natural sciences in principle. It is dealing with the current state, the mature state of a particular organism, namely speakers of English or Japanese or whatever, and it is trying to characterize that state. The characterization of that state will look in some respects like a traditional grammar, but in many ways its concerns are virtually complementary to those of traditional grammar; not entirely, but in large part.

For example, suppose you're writing a teaching grammar—you want to teach Latin or Spanish or something or other. What you will focus on, and what such grammar does focus on, is the idiosyncrasies of that language. So, for example, the grammar had better list all the irregular verbs, and it had better tell you whether verbs precede objects or objects precede verbs and so on. In fact, it had better tell you all of the information about the language which is in fact idiosyncratic, which reflects some sort of parameter in the language system that could be set one way or another. That information has to be given in the grammar, and in fact good grammars do give very extensive lists, in fact comprehensive lists, of idiosyncrasies. All the irregular morphology, for instance, would be listed in any reasonable teaching grammar or classical grammar.

On the other hand, with regard to the regular expressions of the language, the grammar says very little. It may give some examples, but that's all. It will give illustrations saying, "This is a construction, and that's a construction" and so on. But no grammar up until the last twenty-five years even saw that there was a problem. So, for example, if you read, say, some ten-volume grammar of English or German or something like that, it may give you a great deal of information about the regular constructions of English, but the way it gives them to you is by example. It says, "This is a correct sentence," or "This is a relative clause," and so on. Somehow the reader is supposed to be able to look at those examples and figure out what they mean—how they apply to some other construction which wasn't listed in the grammar. At most, informal hints are given to show how other examples are to be formed or interpreted.

Technically speaking, in the case of a traditional grammar such as Jespersen's grammar of English, the coverage is precisely the set of examples that are listed in the grammar. No other example is covered by that grammar, unless you bring to the grammar the intelligence of the reader. Well, that's perfectly reasonable if you're trying to teach a language, let's say; you can presuppose the intelligence of the reader. On the other hand, if you want to understand what the intelligence of the reader is, then you're concerned with precisely what the traditional grammar leaves out, what it presupposes unconsciously. You want to find exactly the set of principles that enables the reader of the grammar to be able to figure out when he sees those examples what the other constructions are, or comparably, that enables a child when he's presented with some sample of experience to develop a system which determines in quite a subtle and precise way the properties, phonetic and semantic and so on, of utterances of his language that are completely unlike any that he's ever heard before. That is the problem, but it is a different problem, and it is virtually complementary to the problem of traditional grammar.

Much of the debate during the fifties and sixties, trying to contrast structuralist and generative grammar, and to fight out the battle of who was right and so on, was almost totally beside the point. I mean, it was like trying to decide what's right, history or physics, or something like that. The point is, they were dealing with totally different questions. I think by now that's basically clear, fortunately.

If you are interested in the questions appropriate to generative grammar, you have a certain research program. If you are interested in some other question, well fine; then you don't have that same research program. The research program you have if you're interested in generative grammar, which is ultimately part of biology, starts with an obvious fact. The fact is that there is something about all of us here in this room which differentiates us from, say, speakers of Swahili. That's some state of our minds. Well, what is that state? Let's give it a name and say it's a steady state that we have attained sometime in childhood. Normally, we attain by, say, puberty, some kind of a steady state with respect to grammar. Our minds have changed up until that point, but they attain a sort of steady state after which changes are very slight. They may be large in terms of, say, the amount of vocabulary we learn, but the properties of the grammar in our minds seem to change very little if at all after that period. We began a some initial state, and we went through a series of states until we reached this state, and this steady state is different for us from that of speakers of Swahili. Of course, these terms themselves are very misleading because as I said the notion "English" doesn't really mean anything very clear. The notion "English" is some sort of political notion, not a linguistic notion. But each of us has in our heads some system, a grammar not a language. Languages are not characteristics of people, grammars are. So we have some grammar in our heads. The grammar in your head is undoubtedly not identical to the one in my head, but close enough so that we can manage. If it is not close enough, we may have trouble. For example, if you come from a very different dialect area than I do our grammars may be virtually identical but nevertheless different enough in their peripheral properties so that we really can't communicate without difficulty. In fact, if you look at the grammar of English and Swahili you are also very likely to find that at some level the grammars are quite similar but different enough, say, in choice of words and so on that people won't be able to communicate.

29

One question in this line of inquiry is to characterize these steady states, to determine their properties. Plainly, the brain is finite, so it is going to contain some finite system which consists of some set of rules and principles which compute and create representations of various kinds and ultimately do it, in fact, for an infinite variety of utterances. This is clear from the surface properties of the problem.

But there is a still more interesting query. Not only is there something about me that is different from a speaker of Swahili, but there is something about both of us that differentiates us from, say, a rock or a bird or a chimpanzee. Some property of our initial state has the characteristic that when it is placed in an environment in which there is use of language it develops the steady state.

The crucial property of the intitial state is that it is a kind of function. You could think of it as a function which takes experience and maps it into the steady state, or, as people sometimes say, it takes data and puts it into a device which is sometimes called universal grammar or a language acquisition device, and ends up giving a grammar. The initial state can be thought of as some kind of an input-output device, some kind of a function, if you like. These are just different ways of stating the same thing. The initial state has the property that under certain conditions set by experience it ends up in a particular state. The problem is to find out what that initial state or input- output device is.

That is the most serious problem of the field, and where the real work is, I think. What we want to ask is, "What are the properties of this system?" Notice that if we had the properties of this system we could explain the facts about our knowledge. Take some fact relating to your and my knowledge of English. For example, if I say, "everyone believes he is intelligent," the sentence can have various interpretations, but one interpretation is something that you might write in logical notation like this: "For every person X, X believes X is intelligent." So, for example, the fact that John believes John is intelligent would be one case of "everybody believes he is intelligent." On the other hand, suppose I make just a minor change in the embedded clause, namely, the most minor change possible: I change it from a finite to an infinitive clause. It comes out "Everybody believes him to be intelligent." Normally, this change yields a sentence synonymous with the original: "Everyone believes John to be intelligent;" "Everyone believes John is intelligent." Those are perfect synonyms. Nevertheless, if I make that trivial change, changing this from a finite to an infinitive clause, the interpretation I gave before is no longer possible. That is, the new sentence, "Everyone believes him to be intelligent" can no longer mean "For every X, X believes X to be intelligent." It has to mean "for every X, X believes somebody else to be intelligent." That's just a fact—that's a datum. We all know that.

All right, that's just a fact about our knowledge. Obviously, nobody was taught that: in fact, up until a couple of years ago nobody even noticed that it was true. So, for example, I doubt if you'll find any teaching grammar or any traditional grammar, however comprehensive, that even mentions that fact—and that makes perfectly good sense. There's no point teaching that, because everybody knows it anyway: It's just a part of our genetic endowment.

Now the question is, what do you know that makes the fact come out that way, despite the absence of teaching, or for that matter the absence of relevant experience. The pattern of explanation seems clear enough: It is to find the properties of the initial state, such that given data that determines that "he" is a pronoun in English and "believes" has the meaning it has, you end up with a grammar which predicts this distinction. The serious work in the field has been devoted to finding principles which present the framework within which knowledge of language develops, whatever the language may be. This framework is then filled out in detail to give you the actual grammar, which yields consequences of the sort just illustrated.

What sort of a system should you end up with? Again, let me stress that while a generative grammar of English will be concerned precisely with examples like the one just given and won't care very much about irregular verbs, a traditional grammar will have exactly the opposite concern. It will be very much concerned with irregular verbs and it won't be concerned at all with things like this. Again, that makes perfect sense. It's not a matter of criticizing one or the other approach. If I were writing a teaching grammar of Spanish, let's say, or teaching Spanish to speakers of English, or the other way around, I would never teach them anything like this because they would know it anyway by virtue of the fact that they were human. For the practical activities of, say, teaching language, it is correct to avoid things of this sort. But, these are precisely the things you want to understand if you are interested in human nature—if you're interested in what it is about humans that enables them to do what we're now doing.

Qualitatively speaking, what kind of a system would you end up with? There are two very striking and obvious facts about language. One is that there is an enormous disparity between the input and the output. That is, the input is extremely impoverished. This example is quite typical: It is extraodinarily unlikely that any of us in our experience has been presented with any evidence at all that tells us that these sentences have the meanings they do. It is conceivable, but very unlikely, and it surpasses belief that all of us were presented with such evidence. In fact, if you try to think of the training program that would be required to give a child that evidence, it would be very hard to do. So what we're stuck with is the enormous disparity between the poverty of the stimulation on the one hand, and the highly articulated and precise character of what comes out, on the order.

Of course, that's a perfectly standard situation in biology. Say somebody is interested in embryological development.

There's something intrinsic, the genetic endowment, and some kind of external environment, say the nutritional environment for the cell or whatever, and some organism results from the interaction—a human being. What everyone assumes in that circumstance is that the growth is internally directed. I don't know if anybody knows much about the actual processes—last time I looked at an encyclopedia of biology they didn't. Maybe they have learned something since, but as of ten years ago when my copy of the encyclopedia came out, nobody knew anything about what makes a human grow arms instead of wings, let's say. Nevertheless, everyone assumed that it was internally directed. That is, if you read the chapter on embryological development, nobody suggested that maybe the embryo tries arms and it tries wings, and arms work out better so it grows arms. That was never proposed because the qualitative properties of the problem tell you that that's the wrong way to go: the environment is much too undifferentiated to account for the highly specific things that take place. If you're rational about it, and you want to look at the question of why humans have arms and not wings, you look in the internal structure. You try to find what it is about the particular coding of information in the genes or whatever that makes a human develop a human visual system rather than an insect visual system.

Quite the same is true here. On the one hand we have this enormous disparity between an undifferentiated and quite impoverished environment and a highly specific state which is attained virtually uniformly for the population across wide differences of intelligence or whatever, and that tells us that there has to be a very rich internal endowment. On the other hand, we see that the languages do differ: English is not Swahili. There have to be some parameters in the system which can be set differently. What we are looking for is a rich system of principles, but one with parameters that can be set one way or another. For example, in English you hear that sentences have the order subject-verb-object, and in some other language, say Japanese, you hear that they have the order subject-object-verb. That means that a parameter has to be fixed somewhere: the object precedes the verb or the verb precedes the object. Or in English you hear sentences like "He eats," and in Italian, sentences like "Mangia," where the "he" isn't expressed; then you simply know that Italian doesn't have to express the subject in places where English does. There are a number of properties of this sort which will differentiate languages, and they have to be in the data. You just have to hear them in the data, but once you hear them the system of principles is fixed. The parameters are fixed, and you have a grammar.

Qualitatively speaking, we know that the existing grammars—what are called existing languages—are very disparate. Nevertheless, they have to be identical at a deeper level. Otherwise, you couldn't learn any of them, because to learn any of them on the basis of the available data you must have a fairly rich fixed system. So we assume that the system of principles is a fairly rich deductive system, with certain parameters to be set by the experience. In a complicated deductive system, if you make a small change here and there the output can be wildly different. In fact, the phenomenon is not unlike speciation, if biologists are now correct. The biochemistry of life looks more or less similar across the whole spectrum, but if you make slight changes, say, in the regulatory mechanisms and timing and so on, you get a totally different organism, because in an intricate enough system, even if it's fixed in character, a little tinkering here and there may make radical differences in output.

That is how language differences look. I mean, it looks as though a few parametric differences, such as the so-called pronoun-drop parameter that differentiates English from Italian, and the order of words and so on, must be fixed by experience, while much else remains constant. This will lead to systems which are very radically different in appearance, although they're all cast from the same mold in a much deeper sense, apart from parametric variations.

That means that so-called language learning is not a matter of finding the principles; you have to learn how to fix the parameters. If we had the right theory, the parameters would be simple enough so that you could learn the values by inspection, from short sentences like "he eats" and "mangia." You would learn from these whether you were speaking a pronoun-drop language or not. If you are speaking a pronoun-drop language, all kinds of things follow because once you feed into this fixed system of properties that this parameter is fixed this way, the range of deductive consequences is quite complex, and it leads to all kinds of things that you never thought of before. Very complicated consequences follow from the fact that a language does or does not have a particular word order, and so on. In a fixed system of principles, changes in those parameters can have a very big and quite complex difference as they proliferate through the system.

I think we're just about getting to the point now—and this I think is rather exciting—where we can put forth theories that begin to have the right properties. Only in the last five or ten years, and particularly in the last two or three years, has it been possible to put forward theories which are qualitatively of the right kind. I don't doubt that they are the wrong theories, but they are of the right kind; that is, they have deductive interconnections of sufficient complexity that when you fix parameters one way or another you get a proliferating chain of consequences through the system, which in some cases turns out to be the right set and in other cases turns out to be the wrong set.

But that's a new stage in the subject. For the first time I think it begins to make it look like a subject that can become assimilated to the natural sciences. Actually, much of the natural sciences isn't like this either. Much of the natural sciences is really classificatory and taxonomic, but there are a few subparts of them where there are explanatory theories, and it seems to me that we can begin to see the day when linguistics could be assimilated to the explanatory part of the natural sciences. That would be exciting if true, and it seems to me that that's more or less where we are now. Why don't I stop at that and we'll talk about anything you like.

Question:

Since we are now getting some idea of the sort of thing a universal grammar should be, the possession of these is unique to humans, and it's carried genetically; and yet the story from biology is that humans have evolved from non-humans. The question is then how something like the universal grammar could have evolved. It seems to be too complicated a thing to be carried on a single pair of genes. In other words, what would an australopithic universal grammar look like, perhaps? Have you thought on this subject?

Chomsky:

Of course that's a different problem. I posed two problems; the reason I posed them is that I think we can look at them seriously. One is the problem of characterizing the steady state; the other is that of characterizing the initial state. Another problem—and that's the one you're talking about—is how to get from the big bang, say, to the initial state, or maybe some piece of this long transition.

Question:

I might clarify my motivation. It seems that at least some chimpanzees have something, and it also seems that what they have isn't like a human universal grammar. So, I wondered if I could understand what they have by trying o figure how human universal grammar could have evolved.

Chomsky:

I suppose it is a bad idea to look at universal grammar to

find out what chimpanzees are like. If you're interested in, say, the insect visual system, you don't study cats; conversely, if you're interested in the cat visual system you don't study bees. Of course, somewhere back far enough, presumably we and lemurs had a common ancestor.

So the question is this: Somewhere within the last ten million years or so, some big things happened which led to humans, which are qualitatively different in some respects from other organisms. What are those things? We can't answer the question in the case of universal grammar; we can't answer it in the case of other human organs. There is a lot of hand-waving about evolution, but we can't begin to answer the question of what happened in human evolution that led to uniquely human characteristics.

Many people say what you said. In fact, many good biologists say it. They say, "Look, there's just not enough information in the genes to determine this, or it's too complex to have arisen through evolution." Those are totally meaningless statements. They are neither true nor false. I mean, how much information is required in the genes to pick up a particular grammar? How much information is required in the genes to pick out two arms rather than three arms? From one point of view, an infinite amount of information is required in the genes to pick out two rather than some other number—but does that mean that having two arms is not genetically determined? Of course not. It just means that that information measure is ludicrous. From an abstract point of view, you need an infinite amount of information to pick out the fact that you have two arms, but that simply tells us that's the wrong measure. You look at something else, at the physics of growth basically, to find out what is going to determine the choice of two arms, given some minuscule fact about the genes, because of the interaction with other factors.

How much information is required to determine that you have a universal grammar? I don't know. Maybe one little change somewhere in human pre-history produced this consequence. One of the few things known about human evolution is that there was a rather explosive growth of brain size, apparently about two million years ago. Maybe there is some unknown physical law that says that when you put ten-to-the-tenth neurons into something the size of a basketball it comes out with transformational grammar. Something vaguely of that nature could be true, for all we know. That's probably how organisms get their properties: Some specific thing happens in a very complex system, and physical laws are such that when that thing happens a lot of other things happen.

Now, sometimes you can even make moderately plausible speculations along these lines. For example, take another fact about humans. You mentioned chimpanzees: Two very striking results have come out from the chimpanzee work, and I think most of the experimenters would agree with this. There has been total failure to get anywhere with chimpanzees in two domains. They can do a lot of things. Dave Premack has his chimpanzees doing very complicated things, figuring out that people have certain intentions. That's pretty complicated. Maybe his conclusion is right or maybe it's wrong, but that is what his data suggest. On the other hand, he has had total failure, as has everyone, in two areas. One is language, and the other is in dealing with numbers. Maybe you can get them to match three things against a series of three things or something like that, but the elementary concept of number, namely that you can add one indefinitely, is apparently incommunicable with the most complicated training system for chimpanzees.

It is an interesting question why humans should have the number faculty. There's a question that could lend itself to evolutionary speculation. Why do humans have a number faculty. Why do we know that you can always add another number? I'm told by anthropologists that if you go into a culture that has no overt number system—maybe 1,2,3, many, but nothing more than that—and you put the people into a market economy, very quickly they know the whole business. They know how to cheat and everything, and they can handle the number system. What that must mean is that this knowledge is sort of just sitting there waiting to be triggered. Well, why? It's very hard to believe that there was any specific selection for it. That is, it is extremely hard to imagine that, say, 20,000 years ago you had more children if you could prove theorems about prime numbers. In fact, there is very little reason to believe that there was any selective effect, so what you'd expect is that it sort of piggybacked on something else. There are some very striking similarities between the number system and the language system. In fact, they both have the property, unique in the whole biological world as far as I know, that they involve discrete infinities.

Take animal communication systems for instance. They are radically different from human language in all sorts of ways. One striking way is that they do not involve the notion of discrete infinity. For example, ape communication systems have some finite number of cries—thirty-six or something. Or, take the bee system: It is really a continuous system, in a way richer than human language. There is variation along a continuous dimension: how much you flap your wings determines what the distance to a good source is, or whatever. But it is actually continuous, in the sense that any physical system can be continuous, infinitely richer than human language.

However, human language has the property of denumerability; there is a denumerable set of expressions. That is also true of the fundamental properties of the number system. We build up with our minds all kinds of other number systems, including continuous ones, but they're ultimately based on the notion of denumerability. It is just possible that what happened is that the mind developed language as a property of neuron packing or something; and given that property, it had the concept of denumerability, so that the number faculty is just hanging around there waiting for the opportunity to come along for us to use it. That could account for both the apparently unique properties of these systems and the fact that apes lack both of them and have no way of dealing with either of them. It seems to me that at that level you can carry out evolutionary speculation, but I don't see how you could speculate much further about the origins of language. People have offered speculations—for example, Harry Jerison. I don't really have any judgment, but they look to me like reasonable speculations about how a predator whose brain was getting bigger in order to catch the smarter and smarter prey would develop a system of imagery, let's say, which would ultimately get inside somewhere instead of being at the peripheral organs, and that might lead to language. Well, maybe.

Question:

There's a difference in the state of mind about puberty between an English speaker and a Swahili speaker; they sort of develop separately. Would bilingual English Swahili be a third state of mind, or a combined state, or is there such a thing as bilingual with your two states of mind? Maybe it's not possible.

Chomsky:

You're pointing to something very important. There are many idealizations in this picture, and one of them is the idea that there is anything like a pure speaker of a language. That's certainly untrue. Every one of us is a multilingual speaker. Every one of us has grown up in some strange mixture of dialects. Our parents spoke one way and our friends spoke a different way, and they spoke a different way on the radio.

The whole idea of one state of mind is already a high level of idealization. Suppose you had an actual homogeneous speech community where all speakers had one system in their minds. Growing up in such a speech community, a child would have a grammar in my sense. But of course no actual child ever grows up in such a community. It doesn't exist. Maybe it exists among the Tasaday, or some group of people who have been alone for the last ten thousand years, but it's so rare that it barely exists. In the real world, everyone grows up in a complex multilingual situation.

This comes back to my first point: that the notion "English" really has no clear meaning. What we call English is something that includes the way you speak and I speak and the way they speak in England and the way they speak in the Ozark Mountains. If there were different political boundaries we might call some of these different languages. The fact of the matter is that all of us are multilingual speakers in the sense that we have some complex of grammars in our heads. Then how do you study that real world situation? Well, I think the way to study it is by trying to separate out its components, one of which is the capacity that every human has to learn language in a homogeneous speech community. Surely everyone has that capacity. To deny that we have it would be to assume something really weird: that the only way to learn language is to be presented with inconsistent data. I don't think anybody believes that. Everyone rational must assume that there is a property of our mind which would allow us to learn language if we were in a homogenous speech community. Now of course, that's not the only property of our mind. We also have other properties, like the ability to learn whatever this thing is in a system of conflicting dialects. To deal with that problem is much harder.

Conflicting languages are just a more extreme version of conflicting dialects, because as I say there really is no difference between dialect and language; it's just a continuum. I mean, it's just a continuum from the difference between you and your mother, which is probably pretty small, to you and the speaker of Swahili, which is pretty large. In between, there's every bit of gradation you like because there's no systematic distinction there. If you take a look at the things that are called "languages" you find that they're very strange. For example, we

41

call German a language, but there are dialects of German that are mutually incomprehensible, and some of them are mutually comprehensible with dialects of what we call Dutch. Or, take Chinese. We call it a language, and we call the parts of it dialects, but they're as different as the Romance languages, more or less.

In fact, the whole business is just a morass. The terms have no clear meaning. There's an old gag everybody learns in the first term of an elementary linguistics course which says that a language is a dialect with an army and a navy.

Language has the same sort of ontological status as a set of behaviors. The set of possible behaviors is not something that's in the world. It is a consequence of what really exists in the world, namely, your physical and mental state. Your physical and mental state determine the set of possible behaviors, but to study the set of possible behaviors would be ridiculous—that's just some superficial epiphenomenon. What you want to study is what it comes from, the components that enter into it, the things that are really there. And the things that are really there are grammars. Of course, in the real world, what you have in your head is not a grammar in this sense. Rather, it is what develops under experience, which is not homogeneous but is rather conflicting. If the experience was so conflicting that it included, say, English and Swahili, you would get some very complicated thing in your head. I don't know what it would be.

Question:

Is there any relationship between the rules of grammar per se and the traditional concept of it that you acquire with the other kind of knowledge required to use the language properly, and if so, would there be a case where you could manipulate a grammar instead of not being able to communicate with somebody else?

Chomsky:

That's a good question. Again, the term "language" is so loose that it covers a variety of sins. If we really started to take it apart, we would find that there are separate elements. What I've been talking about is what you might call the computational part of the language faculty, but there are other factors in what is loosely called language—for example, what you've been talking about. Let's call it the pragmatic system. That's some system of rules that determines how you use language appropriately: You know somehow how to talk to different people in different ways, and you know what to presuppose about what they're saying. People often don't say exactly what they mean. If they did it would be like writing a math proof. Even in mathematics, if you take a look at a proof in a math journal most of it is missing. It's not the case that the conclusion follows from the premises; you presuppose some backgrounds and so on. In normal communication that's going on all the time. We presuppose all sorts of things about the other speaker.

The question you're asking is, "Could the pragmatic system be non-functional while the computational system is functional?" There are clinical cases that suggest that very strongly. Marian Blank, who is in the medical school at Rutgers, I think, has written about this. She has clinical cases of children who appear to be completely competent in the computational side of language, but give the appearance of not being able to speak or understand. Her guess is that somehow they just haven't got under control the set of whatever it is—conventions or principles or whatever—that are involved in normal discourse. Now, it certainly could happen, and maybe her examples indicate that it does happen, but these look like quite separate systems, radically different systems with very different properties.

Question:

Where are linguists looking today to find this universal grammar?

We talked about animal intelligence and comparative dialects, and I can certainly see computers being programmed to produce language. There is activity in the field of biology obviously—but where is one to look?

Chomsky:

Well, you know, research is an opportunistic business. Maybe tomorrow somebody will look somewhere else and that will turn out to be the best place to look, but at the moment, the place to look is in the examples like the ones I gave. It seems to me that the right examples to look at are the cases where we have knowledge, very specific knowledge. After all, the system that emerges results from two factors, what's outside and what's inside. We want to find out what's inside. We're not interested in the linguistic environment; we're interested in the internal system of humans. Therefore, what we will try to look for is ranges of phenomena in which people share very specific and subtle knowledge, but where it is clear that there's very little evidence available on the basis of which they get that knowledge. That will lead us pretty directly to principles that have to be internal. The best to look for the moment is in linguistic data.

Every field has its own properties, and one of the properties of this field is that it is data-rich. All speakers of the language have so much data at their command that you don't have to do experiments. Maybe someday experiments will be useful, but right now if you sit and think for a few minutes, you're just flooded with relevant data that you can't explain.

Well, that's true in the case of your own language. Then there's the work people are doing in the next language, in which they develop principles that are unfortunately often inconsistent with yours; but you know they have to be the same principles because you could have learned that language and they could have learned yours if you had been interchanged in infancy. So that's the next step. If you take a look at a pro-drop language like Italian, it seems to have completely different properties. Even languages that are very close historically, like French and Italian, are radically different in properties. In fact, French is very much like English in many respects, and Italian is very different from both, even though historicially the connections are rather different. The reason is that French doesn't have the pro-drop property and therefore a whole range of things follow in French that are like English. Italian does have the pro-drop property, so a different range of things follows.

A very good research strategy is to take a look at languages like Italian and French, in which the historical depth of their separation is not very great, so you would expect that really radical changes haven't taken place. Nevertheless, if you begin to look at them carefully, you find that they differ systematically in all sorts of ways. It is a good research strategy to take situations like that. I imagine the biological analogue would be the same. If you really want to know about, say, embryological development, it would probably be useful to take two closely related organisms and see how they differ—what makes them come out differently, though we know they are closely related. It is also useful to study radically different languages; for example, some languages of the world apparently hardly use the notion of word order at all.

My colleague, Ken Hale, works on an Australian language called Walbiri, where it appears that you can put the words in virtually any order you like without changing the meaning. Some totally different system appears to be used. It is as if you want to say "The old man saw the brown cow," and you could say "The old brown cow the man saw" or any permutation you like. Now, that language appears to be radically different, but we're certain that it's basically the same, because the Walbiri could have learned English and I could have learned Walbiri, so we can't really be genetically different. There has to be some parameter or some small set of parameters which leads to a wildly different outcome in the two cases. That's a more complex research problem than, say, comparing French and Italian.

You can also look in other areas. For example, it would make good sense to look at empirical studies of language acquisition. Maybe something will be learned by that someday. After all, the study of language acquisition is concerned with the transition from the initial to the steady state, so someday it may provide evidence of some interest. At the moment I don't think it really does. In part, that's sort of an artifact, due to strange historical facts about psychology, which for all sorts of strange reasons has developed as a discipline bent on self-destruction. It often tends to study where you can be fairly certain in advance that you aren't going to learn anything. The study of language acquisition is a case in point.

In studying language acquisition, people often use the following research paradigm. You sit down for several years and you obtain a corpus of data, and you start analyzing it. It's predictable in advance—in fact in this case it was predicted in advance—that the results will be virtually zero. Just as if you tried to do biology, let's say, by taking a motion picture of things happening in the world and saying, O.K., after I've done that for three years I'll sit down and analyze it. The result will be zero. As long as people are going to work in that fashion, you don't even have to bother reading the books. It is inconceivable except by some amazing miracle that they would ever learn anything significant. That's not the way one can ever learn anything. You have to be willing to accept the fact that there are much more abstract principles there somewhere and you've got to design your experimental procedures so that you might shed some light on them. If you insist that all the results must come out of raw data by some sort of inductive procedure, you might as well stay home. Nothing is going to happen.

Perhaps 95 percent of the work in child language acquisition is of that nature; that part doesn't tell you very much. Of the rest—maybe by now the percentage has shifted—about

4 percent is of a different nature, also guaranteed not to produce anything. Namely, that's the study of mother-child interaction. Again, you can predict in advance that the results are
going to be nil. How can you judge in advance? For one thing,
there is the obvious fact that children seem to learn language
virtually equivalently, over quite a broad range, under different
conditions of interaction with the environment. One will learn
language from watching other kids play in nursery school, and
another will learn because he has an overprotective mother
who keeps drilling things into him, but the results are funda-
mentally not very different. So, the investigation of mother-
child interaction is bound to have virtually no consequences,
and in fact it has produced no significant results, predictably.
The reason people do it is that it is easy to do. You can do it if
you know nothing. You don't have to understand anything
about language or children, you just sit there and get data about
the mother-child interaction, analyze the data and publish
books about it. You can be sure that a lot of people are going
to do work of that sort, but it is guaranteed to get nowhere.
Until people are willing to accept the conditions of rational
inquiry, none of this work is going to tell you anything.

Question:
How would you approach research in language acquistion?

Chomsky:
In the case of language acquisition, the rational way to
proceed would be to start by looking at some properties of
language that appear to be universal, or at least significant.
The way to start would be, for example, to see what linguists
have to say about examples like the ones I have mentioned.
No doubt, what they've had to say is wrong, but at least it's
not of zero value: it predicts something. People say, O.K.,
here's the principle which I propose to deal with this example.
Well, that principle has to manifest itself sometime. Alright,

let's see when it manifests itself, and then you can begin to do some work which at least has some relevance to what's going on in the child's mind. For example, you may discover that it's not that principle that manifests itself, but some other one. Well, terrific. Then you would have shown that that was the wrong principle. Or, you may show that the principles seem to manifest themselves as soon as the structures are available—that is, as soon as a child knows that "he" is a pronoun, then the principles are already available.

If that's true, it suggests that the principles really are innate because they are available as soon as it is possible to use them. Lila Gleitman is one of a small number of people who do serious work on language acquisition. Recently she has been working on the language development of blind children. One of the many findings she reported in a recent progress report is that in the area of pronominal reference, they seem to have no lag at all, with the single exception of I and you. They have a slight lag in learning I and you, which if you think about it is quite natural because they don't have the referential basis for it. As far as third person pronominal reference is concerned, they seem to have no lag at all. In particular, in regard to the so-called binding principles that are invovled in the examples I discussed, they seem to function without difficulty. That's of some interest, because blind children of course do have a big deficit in referential support, which you'd think the pronominal system would be concerned with, but it doesn't seem to have much effect.

Many interesting questions could be asked, starting from whatever understanding there is about the system that's acquired. One could then ask how those properties developed or when they developed, and so on. But, in order to do that sort of work, you have to be able to understand the principles, and that requires a little work. It requires that you at least learn what the principles are, or what the evidence suggests that they are. That amount of work is beyond what many experimental psychologists have been willing to do, so they're likely to get results as significant as you would get if you tried to study evolutionary development, refusing to look at what organisms have developed. You're not likely to get very far.

Question:
Is the initial state of language capacity the same for all humans?

Chomsky:
The question you're asking is a special case of a much more general one: whether the initial state is the same for all of us, are some of us genetically predisposed to like one kind of food rather than another, for example. Well, that's just a question of fact. I can't give an answer: I doubt if anyone knows the slightest thing about it. My guess is that it's partly universal; that there are some things that humans will never get to like because of the way they're constructed, or that they'll always like less than other things. And my guess is that an awful lot of it is accidental. The people in a particular culture will tend to like the same things, but if the same child had grown up in another culture, he would have liked some other kinds of things. However, there may be genetic differences. You know, maybe some guy has higher sensitivity for sugar or something so he'll want things with a lower sugar content. These are just questions of fact.

The same is true about the language capacity. I said that the initial state is common to the species. Of course, if we really look in tiny detail, maybe someday we'll be able to find differences among the various initial states. At the moment, such differences as there may be are beyond detection, but that's not to say that they're not there. It may mean that our techniques for detection aren't good enough. My own guess is that people probably differ in this respect as they differ in just about every other respect, but that those differences are just for the moment beyond the capacities for detection.

Somebody asked earlier about research strategies. One kind of research strategy would be to look at the individual differences. The obvious thing to do is to look at the gross ones, say Down's Syndrome or something like that. It is interesting—and people have done some work on it—to see what happens when you have a really gross language deficit. Here's another case: Maureen Dennis in Toronto has been studying a very interesting class of cases of children with complete left hemispherectomy in infancy. That is, the entire left hemisphere of the brain, which more or less controls language, is removed in infancy. It has been thought that their language was normal; that they had complete recovery on the right hemisphere. I'm told that when you talk to those people, they seem to be just like anybody else. However, she began doing some very elementary experiments, really elementary. For example, she looked at how they understood sentences like "John was killed." These are ordinary, simple, passive constructions which involve virtually no computation. It turned out that they were coming out quite different from normals. In a way, this is a genetic defect, I think, which gives an abnormal brain and requires the surgery. So, you don't know whether you're studying the genetic defect, or the effect of having cut out the hemisphere at this early point.

Other things could be looked at. For example, it has apparently been suggested that schizophrenia has a genetic component. Now, there is descriptive work on schizophrenic language. The obvious approach is to take identical twins, one of whom is schizophrenic, and try to look at the non-schizophrenic twin and see if we can find out anything about their language. That's a feasible research project. In fact, in countries like Denmark, where they have good statistics, they apparently know who are the identical twins, one of whom is schizophrenic; and there is a reasonable number of them. Somebody could look at this question, and it could be that you would learn something from such studies of genetic differences that show up in language somehow, as Maureen Dennis's work shows something about differences in brain structure that determine language differences.

If you were going to approach this the way many psychologists have, say, just take a large corpus of the speech of these patients, you would be unlikely to find anything. You must have something in mind that you're looking for, and design circumstances in which that thing will or will not come out. The world is not kind enough to present you with the right data—ever.

References

Blank, Marian. "Mastering the Intangible Through Language." *Annals of the New York Academy of Sciences* 263 (19 Sept. 1975): 44-58.

Descartes, René. *L'homme. Et un traitté De la formation du foetus . . . Avec les remargues de Louis de la Forge . . . our le traitté de l'homme de René Descartes & sur les figures par luy inventées.* Paris, 1664.

Dennis, Maureen. "Dissociated Naming and Locating of Body Parts After Left Anterior Temporal Lobe Resection: An Experimental Case Study." *Brain and Language* 3 (1976): 147-63.

Fodor, Jerry A. *Language of Thought.* New York, 1975.

Fodor, Jerry A. T. G. Bever and M. F. Garrett. *The Psychology of Language: An Introduction to Psycholinguistics and Generative Grammar.* New York, 1974.

Gall, Franz Josef. *Recherchès sur le système nerveux en général et sur celui du serveau en particular.* Paris, 1809.

Hale, Kenneth L. "Gaps in Grammar and Culture." in *Linguistics and Anthropology,* edited by M. Dale Kinkade, Kenneth L. Hale and Oswald Werner. Lisse, 1975.

Jerison, Jerry J. "Paleoneurology and the Evolution of Mind." *Scientific American* 234 (Jan. 1976): 17.

Jespersen, Jens Otto Harry. *A Modern English Grammar on Historical Principles.* 7 vols. London, 1965.

LaForge, Louis de. *Traitté de l'esprit de l'homme, de ses facultez et fonctions, et de son union avec le corps. Suivant les principes de René Descartes.* Paris, 1666.

Marshall, John. "The New Organology." *The Behavioral and Brain Sciences* 3 (1980): 23-25.

Premack, David and Guy Woodruff. "Chimpanzee Problem-Solving: A Test of Comprehension." *Science* 202 (Nov. 1978): 532-35.

3

CHOMSKY BIBLIOGRAPHY

The bibliography that follows has been compiled by means of a systematic search of a wide variety of bibliographic indices which cover the years 1955 (when Chomsky's first publications appeared) through 1982. It is arranged in two large categories: work by Chomsky and work about him.

Works by Chomsky are arranged alphabetically in the following subcategories: books, contributions to anthologies by other editors, articles, introductions and prefaces to works by others, letters to the editor, miscellaneous, and works by him translated into other languages. These latter are further subgrouped into the categories of books (arranged alphabetically under the English-language titles of the individual books), anthologies and articles.

Works about Chomsky are divided into the following categories: books, book reviews, articles, miscellaneous, and works in foreign languages. Book reviews are listed alphabetically by the title of the book. Foreign-language works are further subdivided into the categories of books, articles and book reviews. In all cases, items within categories are arranged alphabetically.

Although the length and variety of the bibliography precluded annotation at this time, occasional notes to specific items provide cross-reference within sections.

By Chomsky

Books

After Pinkville. Boston: New England Free Press, 196?. 12 p.

> Reprinted: *New York Review of Books* 1 Jan 1970, 3-6; also appears as Introduction to "The Conspiracy."

American Power and the New Mandarins. New York: Pantheon Books, 1960. 404 p.

Aspects of the Theory of Syntax. Cambridge: M.I.T. Press, 1965. 251 p.

At War With Asia: Essays on Indochina. New York: Pantheon Books, 1970. 313 p.

> Translations: *Guerre en Asie.*; *La guerra* . . . ; *In krieg.*

The Backroom Boys. London: Fontana, 1973. 222 p.

> Also in: *For Reasons of State.*

Cartesian Linguistics: A Chapter in the History of Rationalist Thought. New York: Harper and Row, 1966. 119 p.

With Edward S. Herman. *Counter-Revolutionary Violence: Bloodbaths in Fact and Propaganda.* Andover, Mass.: Warner Modular Publications, 1973. 46 p.

Current Issues in Linguistic Theory. The Hague: Mouton, 1964. 119 p.

Essays on Form and Interpretation/Noam Chomsky. New York: Elsevier North-Holland, 1977. 216 p.

For Reasons of State. New York: Pantheon Books, 1973, 440 p.

Government and Binding. Dordrecht, Holland: Foris Publication, 1981.

"Human Rights" and American Foreign Policy. Nottingham: Spokes-
man Books, 1978. 90 p.

Language and Mind. New York: Harcourt, Brace and World, 1968.
99 p.

> 2nd ed., revised and enlarged. New York: Harcourt, Brace Jovanovich, 1972.
> 194 p.

Language and Responsibility: Based on Conversations with Mitsou Ronat.
English translation and modification of *Dialogues avec Mitsou
Ronat*, 1977. Translated from the French by John Viertel. New
York: Pantheon Books, 1979. 212 p.; Sussex: Harvester Press,
1979. 212 p.

The Logical Structure of Linguistic Theory. Cambridge, Mass.: M.I.T.
Library, Mimeographed, 1955.

> Reprinted: (Revised edition with an important and informative introduction)
> New York: Plenum Press, 1975. 573 p.

Morphophonemics of Modern Hebrew. Outstanding Dissertations in
Linguistics, edited by Jorge Hankamer, New York: Garland
Publishing, 1979. 74 p.

Peace in the Middle East? Reflections on Justice and Nationhood. New
York: Pantheon Books, 1974. 198 p.

With Edward S. Herman. *The Political Economy of Human Rights.*
Volume I, *The Washington Connection and Third World Fascism;*
Volume II, *After the Cataclysm: Postwar Indochina and the Recon-
struction of Imperial Ideology*. Boston: South End Press, 1979.
441 p., 392 p.

Problems of Knowledge and Freedom. The Bertrand Russell Memorial
Lectures, New York: Pantheon Books, 1971. 111 p.

Reflections on Language. New York: Pantheon Books, 1975. 269 p.

The Responsibility of Intellectuals. Ithaca, N.Y.: Inter-University Committee for Debate on Foreign Policy, 1967?. 12 p.

Reprinted from *New York Review of Books,* February 23, 1967.

Rules and Representations. New York: Columbia University Press, 1980. 299 p.

With Morris Halle. *The Sound Pattern of English.* New York: Harper and Row, 1968. 470 p.

"Studies on Semantics in Generative Grammar". In *Janua Linguarum,* Series Minor, 107. The Hague: Mouton, 1972. 207 p.

Syntactic Structures. The Hague: Mouton, 1957. 118 p.

"Topics in the Theory of Generative Grammar". In *Janua Linguarum,* Series Minor, 56. The Hague: Mouton, 1966. 95 p.

Towards a New Cold War. New York: Pantheon, forthcoming.

A Transformational Approach to Syntax. Cambridge, Mass.: At the University Press, 1958. 54 p.

Reprinted: *Proceedings of the 1958 Conference on Problems of Linguistic Analysis in English,* edited by A. A. Hill. Austin, Texas: 1962. pp. 124-48, and in Fodor and Katz, *The Structure of Language,* 1964.

The Transformational Basis of Syntax. Cambridge, Mass.: Harvard University Press, 1959. 34 p.

Two Essays on Cambodia. Nottingham, England: Bertrand Russell Peace Foundation, 1970. 57 p.

Contributions to Anthologies

With M.P. Schutzenberger. "The Algebraic Theory of Context-free Languages." In *Computer Programming and Formal Systems, Studies in Logic Series,* edited by P. Braffort and D. Hirschbert. Amsterdam: North-Holland, 1963.

"Biological Basis of Language Capacities." In *Psychology and Biology of Language and Thought: Essays in Honor of Eric Lenneberg,* edited by G.A. Miller and E. Lenneberg. New York: Academic Press, 1978.

"The Case Against B.F. Skinner." In *Without/Within: Behaviorism and Humanism,* edited by Floyd W. Matson. Monterey, Calif.: Brooks Cole, 1973.

Chomsky: Selected Readings, edited by J.P.B. Allen and Paul Van Buren.(Language and Language Learning, 31.) London, New York: Oxford University Press, 1971. 166 p.

"Conditions on Transformation." In *Festschrift for Morris Halle,* edited by S.R.Anderson and P. Kiparsky. New York: Holt, Rinehart and Winston, 1973.

"Deep Structure, Surface Structure and Semantic Interpretation." In *Studies in General and Oriental Linguistics,* edited by R. Jakobson and S. Kawamoto. Tokyo: TEC Corporation for Language Research, 1970.

> Reprinted in *Chomsky, Studies on Semantics in Generative Grammar.* 1972, and in *Semantics: An Interdisciplinary Reader in Philosophy, Linguistics and Psychology,* edited by D.O. Steinberg and L.A Jakobovits. Cambridge: At the University Press, 1971.

"Dialogue with Noam Chomsky." In *Discussing Language,* edited by P. Parret. The Hague: Mouton, 1974.

"Explanatory Models in Linguistics." In *Logic, Methodology and Philosophy of Science: Proceedings of the 1960 International Congress,* edited by E. Nagel, P. Suppes and A. Tarski. Stanford, Calif.: Stanford University Press, 1962.

With George A. Miller. "Finitary Models of Language Users." In *Handbook of Mathematical Psychology,* Vol. II, edited by Duncan Luce, Robert R. Bush and Eugene Galanter. New York: John Wiley and sons, 1963.

"Foreign Policy and the Intelligentsia." In *Images and Ideas In American Culture: The Functions of Criticism, Essays in Memory of Philip Rahv,* edited by Arthur Edelstein. Waltham: Brandeis University Press, 1979.

"Formal Discussion: The Development of Grammar in Child Language." In The Acquisition of Language, Monographs of the Society for Research in Child Development, Vol. 29, no. 1. edited by U. Bellugi and R. Brown. Lafayette, Ind.: Purdue University, 1964.

"Formal Properties of Grammars." In *Handbook of Mathematical Psychology,* Vol. II, edited by R. Duncan Luce, Robert R. Bush and Eugene Galanter. New York: John Wiley and Sons, 1963.

"Form and Meaning in Natural Language." In *Communication,* edited by J. D. Roslansky. Amsterdam: North-Holland, 1969.

"The General Properties of Language." In *Brain Mechanisms Underlying Speech and Language,* Proceedings of a Conference held at Princeton, N.J., November 9-12, 1965. P.L. Darley, ed. New York: Grune and Stratton, 1967.

"Introduction: The Linguistic and Psycholinguistic Background." In *Explorations in the Biology of Language,* Papers by the Working Group in the Biology of Language, M.I.T., edited by Edward Walker. Montgomery, Vt.: Bradford, 1978.

With George A. Miller. "Introduction to the Formal Analysis of Natural Languages." In *Handbook of Mathematical Psychology,* Vol. II, edited by R. Duncan Luce, Robert R. Bush and Eugene Galanter. New York: John Wiley and Sons, 1963.

Language and Learning: The Debate Between Jean Piaget and Noam Chomsky, edited by Massimo Piattelli-Palmarini. Cambridge, Mass.: Harvard University Press, 1980.

"Language and Unconscious Knowledge." In *Psychoanalysis and Language, Psychiatry and Humanities 3,* edited by Joseph H. Smith. New Haven: Yale University Press, 1978.

"Linguistics and Philosophy." In *Language and Philosophy,* New York University Institute of Philosophy Symposium, edited by S. Hook. New York: New York University Press, 1969.

Reprinted in Chomsky, *Language and Mind,* 1972.

"Linguistic Theory." In *Northeast Conference on the Teaching of Foreign Languages. Language Teaching: Broader Contexts,* edited by Robert G. Mead, Jr. Northeast Conference on the Teaching of Foreign Languages, 1966 43-49.

"The Logical Basis of Linguistic Theory." In *Proceedings of the Ninth International Congress of Linguistics, Cambridge, Mass., August 27-31, 1962,* edited by Horace G. Lunt. The Hague: Mouton, 1962.

Reprinted in Fodor and Katz, *The Structure of Language as Current Issues in Linguistic Theory,* 1962.

With Morris Halle. "The Morphophonemics of English." In *RLE Quarterly Progress Report No. 58.* Cambridge, Mass.: Massachusetts Institute of Technology, Research Lab. of Electronics, 1960.

With Morris Halle, and F. Lukoff. "On Accent and Juncture in English." In *For Roman Jakobson,* edited by M. Halle, H. Lunt, and MacLean. The Hague: Mouton, 1956.

"On Certain Formal Properties of Grammars." In *Information and Control 2:* 137-67. Reprinted in *Readings in Mathematical Psychology,* Vol. II. edited by R. Duncan Luce, Robert Bush and Eugene Galanter. New York: Wiley, 1963.

"On the Biological Basis of Language Capacities." In *Psychology and Biology of Language and Thought: Essays in Honor of Eric Len-*

neberg, edited by George A. Miller and Elizabeth Lenneberg. New York: Academic, 1978.

"On the Nature of Language." In *Origins and Evolution of Language and Speech,* Annals of the New York Academy of Sciences, 280, edited by Steven R. Harnad, Horst d. Steklis, and June Lancaster. New York: Academy of Sciences, 1976.

"On the Notion 'Rule of Grammar.'" In *Structure of Language and Its Mathematical Aspects,* Proceedings 12th Symposium in Applied Mathematics, edited by R. Jakobson. Providence, Rhode Island: American Mathematical Society, 1961.

> Reprinted in Fodor & Katz, *The Structure of Language.*

"On Wh-Movement." In *Formal Syntax,* Papers from the MSSB-UC Irvine Conference on the Formal Syntax of Natural Language, Newport Beach, Calif.: 1976, edited by Peter W. Culicover, Thomas Wascow, and Adrian Akmajian. New York: Academic Press, 1977.

"Perception and Language." In *Boston Studies in the Philosophy of Science,* edited by Wartofsky. Dordrecht, Holland: Reidel, 1963.

"Phonology and Reading." In *Basic Studies in Readings,* edited by Harry Levin and Joannea P. Williams. New York: Basic Books, 1970.

"Problems of Explanation in Linguistics." In *Explanations in the Behavioural Sciences,* edited by R. Borger and F. Cioffa. New York: Cambridge University Press, 1970.

"Questions of Form and Interpretation." In *The Scope of American Linguistics,* Papers of the First Golden Anniversary Symposium of the Linguistic Society of America, Held at the University of Massachusetts, Amherst, on July 24-25, 1974, edited by Robert Austerlitz. Lisse: De Ridder, 1975.

"Quine's Empirical Assumptions." In *Synthese*. 19 (1968): 53-68. Reprinted in *Words and Objections*, edited by D. Davidson and J.Hintikka. Dordrecht, Netherlands: Reidel, 1969.

Eric H. Lenneberg, George Miller, et. al. *Readings in Applied Transformational Grammar*, edited by Mark Lester. New York: Holt, Rinehart and Winston, 1970. 314 p.

Remarks on Nominalization. Bloomington, Ind.: Linguistics Club, Indiana University, 1968.

> Reprinted in *Readings in Transformational Grammar*, edited by R. Jacobs and P. Rosenbaum. Waltham, Massachusetts: Ginn and Co, 1970; and in Chomsky, *Studies in Generative Grammar*, 1972.

"Some Empirical Assumptions in Modern Philosophy of Language." In *Philosophy, Science and Method*, edited by S. Morgenbesser. New York: St. Martin's Press, 1969.

"Some Empirical Issues in the Theory of Transformational Grammar." In *Goals of Linguistic Theory*, edited by S. Peters. Englewood Cliffs, N.J.: Prentice-Hall, 1972.

> Reprinted in Chomsky, *Studies on Semantics in Generative Grammar*, 1972.

"Some Observations on the Problems of Semantic Analysis in Natural Languages." In *Sign, Language, Culture*, edited by A.J. Griemas, R. Jakobson, M.R. Mayenowa, S.K. Saumjan, W. Steinitz, and S. Zolkiewski. The Hague: Mouton, 1970.

Trials of the Resistance: Essays by Noam Chomsky and Others. New York: New York Review, 1970. 246 p.

Articles

"After Pinkville, What?" *Current* 115 (1970): 18-30.
> Excerpts from *After Pinkville*, The *New York Review of Books*, 1 January 1970.

"Armageddon Is Well Located." *Nation* 22 July 1978, 83-88.

With Edward S. Herman. "Benign Terror-East Timor." *Bulletin of Concerned Asian Scholars,* (1979): 40.

"Breaking the Mideast Deadlock: II The Prospects." *Ramparts* April, 1975, 31-33.

"Business and Society Review Misses the Point." *Business and Society Review* 25 (Spring 1978): 17.

"Cambodia: A Special Supplement." *New York Review of Books* 4 June 1970, 39-50.

"The Carter Administration: Myth and Reality." *Australian Quarterly,* 50 (March 1978): 8-36.

"Chomsky on Kripke." *New York Times* 14 August 1977, VI, 20.

"A Communication." *New Republic* 23 November 1974, 56-7.

"Conditions on Rules of Grammar." *Linguistic Analysis* 2 (1976): 303-51.

>   Reprinted in *Current Issues in Linguistic Theory.* Distinguished Lecture Series, 1975 Linguistic Institute. Roger W. Cole, ed. Bloomington: Indiana University Press, 1977. 303 p.

"Context-free Grammars and Pushdown Storage." In *RLE Quarterly Progress Report No. 65.* Cambridge, Mass.: Massachusetts Institute of Technology, 1962.

"The Crisis Managers." *New York Times* 25 June 1971, 35.

"The Current Scene in Linguistics: Present Directions." *College English* 27 (1966): 587-95.

>   Reprinted in *Modern Studies in English,* edited by D.A. Reibel and S.A. Schane. Englewood Cliffs, N.J.: Prentice-Hall, 1969.

"Current Scene in Linguistics: Present Directions-Reply." *College English* 28 (1967): 468-69.

"Czechoslovakia Hypocrisy." *Index* 4 (Spring 1975): 74-76.

With Edward S. Herman. "Distortions at Forth Hand." *Nation* 25 June 1977, 789-98.

"Endgame: The Tactics of Peace in Vietnam." *Ramparts* April 1973, 26-9.

"Equality: Language Development, Human Intelligence and Social Organization." *Philosophy and Social Action* 2 (July-September 1976): 1-20.

"Essays in Linguistics." Review of Greenberg, *Essays in Linguistics*. Word 15 (1959): 202-18.

"The Fallacy of Richard Hernstein's I.Q." *Social Policy* 3 (1972): 19-25.

"The Faurisson Affair: His Right to Say It." *Nation* 232 (1981), 231-4.

With Howard Lasnik. "Filters and Control." *Linguistic Inquiry* 8 (1977): 425-504.

With George A. Miller. "Finite State Languages." *Information and Control* 1 (1958): 91-112.

> Reprinted in Readings in Mathematical Psychology, Vol. 2, edited by Duncan Luce, Robert R Bush and Eugene Gallanter. New York: Wiley, 1963, 156-57.

"Fundamentals of Language." Review of Jakobson and Halle. *International Journal of American Linguistics* 23 (1957): 234-42.

"Hernstein Response." *Cognition* 1 (1972): 407-18.

"His Right to Say It." *Nation* 28 February 1981, 231-34.

"Indochina: The Next Phase." *Ramparts* May 1972, 14.

"In North Vietnam." *New York Review of Books* 13 August 1970, 16.

"Intolerable Evils Justify Civil Disobedience." *New York Times* 26 November 1967, VI, 27.

"I. Q. Tests: Building Blocks for the New Class System." *Ramparts* July 1972, 24-25.

"Israel and the Palestinians." *Social Revolution* 5 (1975): 45-86.

Review of "Just and Unjust Wars" by Michael Walzer. *Australian Outlook* 32 (1978): 357-63.

"Knowledge of Language." Excerpted from the first John Locke Lecture, Oxford University, 29 April 1969. *Times Literary Supplement* (London) 68 (1969): 523-5.

> Reprinted in *Minnesota Studies in Philosophy of Science*, Vol. VI, edited by K. Gunderson and J. L. Maxwell. Minneapolis: University of Minnesota Press, 1975.

"Language and Freedom" *Abraxas* 1 (1970): 9-24, and *Tri Quarterly* 23-24 (1972): 13-33.

"Linguistics, Logic, Psychology and Computers." Lectures given at University of Michigan, 1948. *Computer Programming and Aertifical Intelligence*, 1958, pp. 429-56.

"Logical Structures in Language." *American Documentation* 8 (1956-1957): 284-91.

"Logical Syntax and Semantics: Their Linguistic Relevance." *Language* 31 (1955):36-55.

"Manual of Phonology." Review of Hockett. *International Journal of American Linguistics* 23 (1957): 223-34.

"The Mideast: Dark at the End of the Tunnel." *Ramparts* January 1973, 38-40.

"The Mideast War: II The Background." *Ramparts* January 1974, 37-9.

"National Interest and the Pentagon Papers." *Partisan Review* 3 (1972): 336-54.

"Nature of Language." *Annals of the New York Academy of Sciences* 280 (1976): 46-57.

"The New Organology." *Behavioral and Brain Sciences* 3 (1980): 42-58.

With Stuart Hampshire. "Noam Chomsky and Stuart Hampshire Discuss the Study of Language." *Listener* 79 (1968): 687-91.

"A Note on Phrase Structure Grammars." *Information and Control* 2 (1959): 393-95.

"Notes on Anarchism." *New York Review of Books* 21 May 1970, 30-35.

"On Binding." *Linguistic Inquiry,* 11 (Winter 1980): 1-46.

"On Civil Disobedience." *New York Times Magazine* 26 November 1967, 27-8.

With J.J. Katz. "On Innateness." *Philosophical Review* 84 (1974): 347-67.

"On Innateness: A Reply to Cooper." *Philosophical Review* 84 (1975): 70-87.

"On Trusting Experts Too Much." *Psychology Today* 12 (May 1979): 35.

"Philosophers and Public Philosophy: A Symposium." *Ethics* 79 (October 1968): 1-9.

"Plight of East Timor." *Australian Quarterly* 5 (March 1979): 47-61.

"Prospects for Settlement of Israeli-Arab Conflict." *Denver Journal of Inquiry* 5 (1975): 393-400.

"Psychology and Idealogy." *Cognition* 1 (1972): 11-46.

"Recent Contributions to the Theory of Innate Ideas." *Synthese* 17 (March 1967): 2-11.

"Reflections on the Arab-Israeli Conflict." *Journal of Contemporary Asia* 5 (1975): 337-44.

"Remaking of History." *Ramparts* August 1975, 30-33.

With Howard Lasnik. "A Remark on Contraction." *Linguistic Inquiry* 9 (1978): 268-74.

"Reporting Indochina: The News Media and the Legitimation of Lies." *Social Policy* 4 (1973): 4-20.

"Response to Sidney Hook." *Humanist* 31 (1971): 23-9.

"Response to Sidney Hook II." *Humanist* 31 (1971): 30-4.

"Revolt in the Academy: Some Thoughts on the Student Movement." *Modern Occasions* 1 (1970): 53-75.

"The Rule of Force in International Affairs." *Yale Law Journal* 80 (June 1971): 1456-91.

With Edward S. Herman. "Saigon's Corruption Crisis: The Search for An Honest Quisling." *Ramparts* December 1974, 21-24.

Semantic Considerations in Grammar. Monograph No. 8. Washington, D.C.: Georgetown University Institute of Languages and Linguistics, 1955.

"Should Traditional Grammar Be Ended or Mended?" *Educational Review* 22 (1969): 5.

With Morris Halle. "Some Controversial Questions in Phonological Theory." *Journal of Linguistics* 1 (1965): 97-138.

"Some General Properties of Phonological Rules." *Language* 43 (1967): 102-28.

"Some Methodological Remarks on Generative Grammar." *Word* 17 (1961): 219-39.

"Some Observations on the Teaching of Language." *The Pedagogic Reporter* 21 (1969): 5-6.

"Some Thoughts on Intellectuals and the Schools." *Harvard Educational Review,* 36 (1966): 484-91.

"The Student Movement." *Humanist* 30 (September-October 1970): 19-25.

"Systems of Syntactic Analysis." *Journal of Symbolic Logic* 18 (1953): 242-56.

"Three Models for the Description of Language." *I.R.E. Transactions on Information Theory.* IT-2 (1965): 113-24.

> Reprinted in *Readings in Mathematical Psychology,* Vol. 2, edited by R. Duncan Luce, Robert Bush and Eugene Galanter, 105-24. New York: Wiley, 1965.

"United States Media and TET Offensive." *Race and Class* 20 (1978): 21-39.

With Edward S. Herman. "The United States Versus Human Rights in the Third World." *Monthly Review* July 1977, 22-45.

"A Universal Grammar: A Discussion with Stuart Hampshire and Alasdair MacIntyre." *The Listener* 30 May 1968, 1-6.

"Verbal Behavior." Review of B.F. Skinner. *Language* 35 (1959): 26-58.

With Hans J. Morgenthau and Michael Walzer. "Vietnam and Cambodia." *Dissent* 25 (1978): 386-91.

With Lionel Abel. "Vietnam, the Cold War and Other Matters." *Commentary* October 1969, 12-43.

"Waiting for Lefty: Excerpt from *Language and Responsibility*." *Nation* 27 January 1979, 77-81.

"Watergate and Other Crimes." *Ramparts* June 1974, 31-6.

"Welfare-Warfare Intellectuals." *New Society* 14 (1969): 12-6.

"Western Press and Cambodia." *Journal of Contemporary Asia* 7 (1977): 548-54.

With Jerrold J. Katz. "What the Linguist is Talking About." *Journal of Philosophy* 71 (1974): 347-67

"Who Believes in Ghosts?" *Newsweek* 26 August 1968, 55-6.

With Edward S. Herman. "Why American Business Supports Third World Facism." *Business and Social Review* 23 (Fall 1977); 13-21.

Introduction/Preface to Works by Others

Introduction to *Anarchism: From Theory to Practice* by Daniel Guérin, vii-xx. Translated by Mary Klopper. New York: Monthly Review Press, 1970,

"Forward" to *The Arabs in Israel* by Sabri Jiryis. New York: Monthly Review Press, 1976.

With Otto Marx. "The Formal Nature of Language." Appendix to *Biological Foundations of Language* by Eric H. Lenneberg. New York: John Wiley and Sons, 1967.

Reprinted in 1972 edition of Chomsky, *Language and Mind.*

"Preface" to *Cambodia in the Southeast Asian War* by Malcolm Caldwell and Lek Tan. New York: Monthly Review Press, 1973.

"Introduction" to *Cointelpro: The FBI's Secret War on Political Freedom,* edited by Cathy Perkus. New York: Monad Press, 1976.

"Introduction" to *The Conspiracy* by Abbie Hoffman, Bobby Seale, Rennie Davis, David Dellinger, John Froines, Tom Hayden, Jerry Rubin, and Lee Weiner, edited by Peter Babcock, Deborah Babcox, and Bob Abel. New York: Dell Publishing Co., 1969.

"Preface" to *Introduction to Formal Grammars,* by Maurice Gross and André Lentin. Translated by M. Salkoff. Heidelberg: Springer, 1970.

"Introduction" to Adam Schaff, *Language and Cognition,* edited by Robert S. Cohen. Based on Tr. by Olgierd Wojtasiewicz. New York: McGraw-Hill.[Tr. Jezyk a poznanie, Warsaw, 1964.]

"Introduction" to *Memoire en Defense* by Robert Faurisson. Paris: La Vieille Toupe, 1980.

See Edger, Richard. "Chomsky: Faurisson Affair-His right to Say It," below (About Chomsky, Articles).

"Introduction" to *Open Secret: The Kissinger-Nixon Doctrine in Asia,* edited by Virginia Brodine and Mark Selden. New York: Harper and Row (Perennial Library) 1972.

Letters to the Editor

With A. Mayer, R. Poirier, S.E. Luria, R. Falk, S. Sontag, R.P. Wolff and R. Heilbroner. "Ban on Ernest Mandel." *New York Times* 25 October 1969, 32.

"Cambodia." *New York Review of Books* 18 June 1970, 43.

"Cambodia Year Zero." *Times Literary Supplement* 4 January 1980, 14.

"Cambodia Year Zero." *Times Literary Supplement* 15 February 1980, 177.

"Chomsky Protests La Couture Falsehoods." *Encounter* October 1979, 93-4.

"The Conscience of Yugoslavia." *New York Review of Books* 7 January 1971, 42.

"Exchange of Views on Language and Human Values." *Encounter* 49 (1977): 93-4.

Robert S. Cohen and Howard Zinn. "Father Berrigan's Actions." *New York Times* 23 August 1970, IV, 13.

"Future of Israel." *Commentary* 59 (1975): 4-9.

"Holocaust Agnostic." *New Republic* 14 February 1981, 5.

With Edward S. Herman. "Langguth Misread Us." *Nation* 230 (1980): 770.

"The Middle-East and the Intellectuals." *Commentary* October 1970, 13-4.

"Moscow vs a Linguist." *New York Times* 10 April 1976, 26.

"Noam Chomsky and Cambodia." *International Affairs* October 1979, 595-96.

"Policies on War." *Washington Post* 11 March 1977, A: 24.

"Protest From Israel." *New York Review of Books* 24 (1977): 46.

"Quotable Truman." *Commentary* 49 (1970): 14.

With F. Schurman. "Radical Journal." *Humanist* 30 (1970): 46.

With I.F. Stone. "Repression in Belgrade." *New York Times,* 11 December 1973, 44.

With Stanley Hoffman and John Kenneth Galbraith. "Repression in Belgrade." *New York Times* 18 March 1973, IV, 12.

With John T. Edsall, Paul A. Saumelson, H. Eugene Stanley, and Charles H. Townes. "Soviet Pressure." *New York Times* 5 January 1975, IV, 16.

With Mark Sacharoff, Robert Jay Litton, and Fred Branfman. "Strategy in Indochina." *New York Times* 16 February 1972, 38.

With S. E. Luria. "A U.S. Debt to Iran." *New York Times* 2 May 1980, 26.

"The Truman Speech." *Commentary* 49 (1970): 4.

With S.E. Luria. "A U.S. Debt to Iran." New York Times 2 May 1980, 26.

Miscellaneous

Brain Science Briefings. Sound recording. Plainville, N.Y.: Ferranti Electric, 1974.

With Howard Zinn, eds. Critical Essays and an Index to *The Pentagon Papers: The Defense Department's History of United States Decision Making on Vietnam.* The Senator Gravel Edition. 5 vols. Boston: Beacon Press, 1971-72.

Government in the Future. Sound recording. New York: Jeffrey Norton Publishers, 1970. 57 min.

An Interview with Noam Chomsky. Sound recording. New York: Harper & Row, 1973.

"Transformational Analysis." Ph.D. dissertation, University of Pennsylvania, 1955.

Two Transformational Grammars. [Taipei?] English Teachers Retraining Project, Taiwan Provincial Normal University [in association with] University of Texas [and] Agency for International Development, 1964.

Translated and Foreign-language Works

Books

American Power and the New Mandarins.

Die Verantwortlichkeit der Intellektuellen. Translated by Anna Kamp. Frankfort: Suhrkamp, 1971. 205 p.

El pacifismo revolucionario. Selections from *American Power and the New Mandarins.* Translated by Elsa Cecilia Frost. Mexico: Siglo Veintiuno Editorial, 1973. 117 p.

L'Amérique et ses Nouveaux Mandarins. Translated by Jean-Michel Jasienko. Paris: Editions du Seuil, 1969. 334 p.

Aspects of the Theory of Syntax.

Aspectos del la teoria de la sintaxis. Introducción, versión, notas y apéndice de C.P. Otero. Madrid: Aguilar, 1970. 260 p.

Aspects de la Théorie Syntaxique. Translated by Jean Claude Milner. Paris: Editions du Seuil, 1971. 283 p.

Aspekte der Suntax-theorie. Frankfort: Suhrkamp Verlag, 1969. 313.

Aspekty Teorii Sintaksisa. Translated by V.A. Zvengintseva. Moscow: Izd-vo Moskovskogo University, 1972. 258 p.

At War with Asia.

Guerre en Asie. Translated by Martine Laroche. Paris: Hachette, 1971. 383 p.

Im Krieg mit Asien. Frankfort: Suhrkamp, 1972.

La guerra americana in Asia; Saggi Sull 'Indocina. Torion: G. Einaudi, 1972. 358 p.

Cartesian Linguistics.

La Linguistsique Cartesienne: Un Capitre de Histoire de la Pensée Rationaliste Suive de la Nature Formelle du Langage. Paris: Editions du Seuil, 1969. 182 p.

Linguistica cartesiana: Un capítulo de la historia del pensamiento racionalista. Translated by Enrique Wulff. Madrid: Editorial Gredos, 1969. 158 p.

Counter-Revolutionary Violence.

With Edward S. Herman. *Bains de Sang Contructifs: Dans les Faits et la Propagande.* Translated by Mari-Odile et Jean Pierre Faye. Paris: Editions Seghers/Laffont, 1975. 195 p.

Dialogues Avec Mitsou Ronat.

Dialogues Avec Mitsou Ronat. Paris: Flammarion, 1977. 210 p.

Formal Analysis of Natural Language.

With George A. Miller. *El análisis formal de los lenguajes naturales.* Translated by Carlos Piera. Madrid: Comunicación, 1972. 145 p.

With George A. Miller. *L'analisi formale del linguaggio.* Turin: Boringhieri, 1969.

With George A. Miller. *L'analyse formelle des langues naturelles.* Translated by P. Richard and N. Ruwet. The Hague: Mouton, 1968. 180 p.

Language and Mind

El lenguage y el entendimiento. Translated by Juan Feraté. Barcelona: Editorial Seix Barral, 1971.

Le langage et la pensée. Translated by Louis-Jean Calvet. Paris: Payot, 1970.

Sprache und Geist. Frankfurt: Suhrkamkp, 1969.

Taal en Mens. Tr. by A. Kraak. Deventer: Van Loghum Slaterus.

Problems of Knowledge and Freedom.

Conocimiento y libertad. Barcelona: Ariel, 1972. 187 p.

Responsibility of the Intellectuals.

A responsabilidade dos intelectuais. Translated by Maria Luísa Pinheiro e Ella Gibson. Lisbon: Publicacões Dom Quixote, 1968. 107 p.

Sobre la responsabilidad de los intelectuales. Havana, Cuba: Casa de las Américas, 1968.

Sound Pattern of English

With Morris Halle. *Principes de phonologie Générative.* Translated by Pierre Encrevé. Paris: Editions du Seuil, 1973. 348p. (1st and 4th part of *The Sound Pattern of English*).

Syntactic Structures.

Estructuras sintácticas. Mexico: Siglo Veintiuno Editores, 1975.

Gramatika i um / Noam Comski. Translated by Ranko Bugarski. Belgrade: Nolit, 1972.

Syntaktiché struktury. Praha, Academia, 1966.

Structures Syntaxiques. Translated by Michel Braudeau. Paris: Seuil, 1969. 140 p.

Strukturen der Syntax. The Hague: Mouton, 1973. 136 p.

Syntactic Structures. Translated into Korean by Seung-hwan Lee and Hei-sook Lee. Seoul, Korea: Pan-Korea Book Corp., 1966.

Foreign-language Anthologies

"Einige empirische Annahmen in der Moderen Sprachphilosophie". In *Linguistik und Philosophie,* edited by Günther Grewendorf and Georg Meggle. Frankfurt: Anthenäum, 1974.

"Linguistik und Philosophie". In *Linguistik und Philosophie,* edited by Günther Grewendorf and Georg Meggle. Frankfurt: Athenäum, 1974.

Tiefenstruktur, Oberflächenstruktur und Semantische Interpretation." In *Aspekte der Semantik. Zu Ihrer theorie und Geschichte 1662-1970,* edited by Laszlo Antal. Frankfurt: Athenäum, 1972.

Foreign-language Articles and Essays

"De quelques constantes de la théorie linguistique." *Diogéne,* June-September 1965, 51: 14-21.

Intellectuals and the State = De Intellectuelen en de Staat. Johan Huizinga lecture, Leiden, December, 1977. Baarn, The Netherlands: Internationale, Het Wereldvenster, 1978.

Reprinted in *Freedom* 39:7 (April, 1978): 9-17.

"Interpretar, cambiar el mundo." *Plural : Crítica, Arte, Literatura,* 3(1971): 3-12; 4(1972), 33-39.

"Langage des machines et langage humain." (Review of Belevitch). *Language* 34 (1958): 99-105.

"Recensión Crítica de 'Verbal Behavior' de B. F. Skinner." *Convivium* 38 (1973): 65-106.

Saggi Linguistici / Noam Chomsky; La Cura Redazionale è di Armando de Palma. Translated by Armando de Palma et al. Turin: Boringhieri, 1969-1970.

(Review of) "White-House Years", by Henry Kissinger (Italian). *Ponte Rivista Mensile Di Politica E Letteratura* 36 (1980): 683-708.

About Chomsky

Books

Coutler, Jeff. *The Social Construction of Mind: Studies in Ethomethodology and Linguistic Philosophy.* Totowa, N.J.: Rowman Littlefield, 1979.

Davis, Steven. *Philosophy and Language.* Indianapolis: Bobbs-Merrill, 1976.

Dinneen, Francis P. *An Introduction to General Linguistics.* New York: Holt, Rinehart and Winston, 1967.

Gardner, Howard. *The Quest For Mind: Piaget, Levi-Strauss and the Structuralist Movement.* New York: Knopf, 1972.

Greene, Judith. *Psycholinguistics: Chomsky and Psychology.* Baltimore, Md.: Penguin Books, 1972.

Harman, Gilbert, ed. *On Noam Chomsky: Critical Essays.* Garden City, N.Y.: Anchor Press, 1974. 348p.

Harrison, Bernard. *Meaning and Structure: An Essay In the Philosophy of Language.* New York: Harper and Row, 1972.

Hiroth, Finngeir. *Noam Chomsky, Lingusitics and Philosophy.* Oslo Universit Etsforlaget, 1974.

Book Review: J. Miller *Journal of Linguistics* 12(1976): 192-199.

Katz, Jerrold J. *The Philosophy of Language.* Noam Chomsky and Morris Halle, ed. New York: Harper and Row, 1966.

———. *Semantic Theory.* New York: Harper and Row, 1972.

——— and Paul M. Postal. *An Integrated Theory of Linguistic Descriptions.* Cambridge, Mass. MIT Press, 1964.

Lawrence, Irene. *Linguistics and Theology: The Significance of Noam Chomsky for Theological Construction.* Metuchen, N.J.: Scarecrow Press, 1980.

Leiber, Justin. *Noam Chomsky A Philosophic Overview.* New York: Twayne Publishers, 1975.

Lyons, John. *Noam Chomsky.* 2d rev. ed. New York: Penguin, 1970.

Matthews, Peter H. *Generative Grammar and Linguistic Competence.* London, Boston: G. Allen and Unwin, 1979.

Mehta, Ved Parkash. *John is Easy to Please: Encounter with the Written and Spoken Word.* New York: Farrar, Straus and Giroux, 1971.

Olmested, David Lockwood. *Heresy in Linguistics.* Davis, CA.: University of California Library. Chapbook No. 3, 1975.

Robinson, Ian. *The New Grammarians' funeral: A Critique of Noam Chomsky's Linguistics.* Cambridge: At the University Press, 1975.

Ryle, Gilbert. *On Thinking.* Konstantin Kolenda, ed. Totowa, N.J.: Rowman Littlefield, 1979. 136p.

Sampson, Geoffrey. *Liberty and Language.* Oxford: Oxford University Press, 1979.

Sampson, Geoffrey. *Making Sense.* Oxford: Oxford University Press, 1980.

———. *Stratificational Grammar A Definition and an Example.* The Hague: Mouton, 1970.

Seuren, Pieter A.M. *Operators and Nucleus: A Contribution to the Theory of Grammar.* Cambridge: At the University Press, 1969.

Smith, Neil and Deirdre Wilson. *Modern Linguistics the Result of Chomsky's Revolution*. Bloomington Indiana University Press, 1979.

Stich, Stephen P., ed. *Innate Ideas*. Los Angeles: University of California Press, 1975.

Stringer, David. ed. *Generative Linguistics: An Introduction to the Work of Noam Chomsky*. Bletchley, England: University Press, 1973.

Book Reviews

American Power and the New Mandarins

Clark, Collin. "The Contemporary Scene." *Library Journal* 15 February 1969, 740.

Deutsch, Jan G. "American Power and the New Mandarins." *New York Times* 16 March 1969, VII:1.

Dornan, J.E. Jr. "Books in Brief." *National Review* 21(1969): 607.

Duberman, Martin. "Immoral Imperialism." *New Republic*, 12 April 1969, 27-30.

Flew, Anthony. "New Left isolationism." *Humanist* 31 (1971): 38-40.

Gross, Robert A. "The Corridors of Power." *Newsweek*, 24 March 1969, 104.

Hamilton, William. "The Left: Neither Gauche nor Sinister." *Christian Century*, 23 July 1969, 995.

Harrison, Joseph G. "Chomsky's War: Bombing the Establishment." *Christian Science Monitor*, 3 April 1969, 15.

Harrison, Joseph G. "Mandarins and Motives." *Economist,* 29 November 1969, 59.

Harvard, William C. "A New Rousseau." *Virginia Quarterly Review,* 45(1969):509.

Kearny, Vincent S. "World Scene." *America* 120 (1969):546.

Konvitz, Milton R. "War: American Power and the New Mandarins, Historical and Political Essays." *Saturday Review,* 31 May 1969, 26.

Schlesinger, Arthur Jr. "American Power and the New Mandarins." *Book World,* 23 March 1969, 4.

———. "American Power and the New Mandarins." *Choice* 6 (1969): 1266.

Sklar, Robert. "The Intellectual Power Elite." *Nation* 208 (1969): 373-374.

Arabs in Israel

Stern, Sol. "The Arabs in Israel." *New York Times Book Review,* 25 July 1976, 4.

Rubenstein, Alviz Z. "The Arabs in Israel." *Current History,* 72 (1977): 28.

Aspects of Theory of Syntax

Contreras, Heles. "Book Reviews." *Modern Language Journal.* February 1967, pp. 110-111.

Ferebee, Ann S. "Aspects of the Theory of Syntax." *Journal of Symbolic Logic* 35 (1970): 167.

Harman, Gilbert H. "Chomsky's Theory of Syntax: Two Review Articles. 'Psychological Aspects of the Theory of Syntax.' "*Journal of Philosophy* 64 (1967): 75-87.

Hiz, Henry. "Chomsky's Theory of Syntax: Two Review Articles. 'Methodological Aspects of the Theory of Syntax.' " *Journal of Philosophy* 64 (1967): 67-74.

Jacobsin, Sven. "Review of Chomsky: Aspects of the Theory of Syntax." *Linguistics* 28 (1966): 111.

Lyons, John. "Aspects of the Theory of Syntax." *Philosophical Quarterly* 16 (1966): 393.

Matthews, Peter H. "Aspects of the Theory of Syntax." *Journal of Linguistics* 3 (April 1967): 119-151.

Ohman, Richard. "The Theory of Talk." *Partisan Review,* 32:3 (Summer 1965): 457-461.

Peng, Fred C.C. "Aspects of the Theory of Syntax." *Linguistics,* No. 49 (1969), pp. 91-127.

Peter, Harry Winfield. "Reviews." *Modern Language Review* 63 (1968): 132-133.

Plochmann, George Kimball. "Aspects of the Theory of Syntax." *Philosophy and Phenomenological Research* 28 (1967): 278.

Reno, Edward A. Jr. "Summaries and Comments." *Review of Metaphysics* 19 (1966): 806.

Staal, J.F. "Reviews." *Journal of Symbolic Logic* 32 (1967): 385-387.

At War With Asia

"At War With Asia." *Virginia Quarterly Review* 47 (1971).

Barkmann, Charles Lam. "At War With Ourselves." *Nation* 212 (1971): 633.

Morgenthau, Hans J. "At War With Asia: That Our Presence in Vietnam is Unwise, Absurd and Wrong." *New York Times Book Review* 17 January 1971, VII, 22.

Osborne, Milton E. "At War With Asia." *Pacific Affairs* 44 (1971): 309.

Powell, Enoch J. "America's Moral Egocentrism." *New York Times,* 1 March 1971, 29.

Windsor, Philip. "What's Left of American Liberalism?" *Listener* 85 (1971): 182-83.

Cartesian Lingustics

"Babel and After: Society and the Structure of Language." *Times Literary Supplement* 10 November 1966, 1022.

Bracken, Harry M. "Chomsky's Variations on a theme by Descartes." *Journal of the History of Philosophy* April 1970, 181.

Brekle, Herbert E. "Review of Chomsky, *Cartesian Linguistics.*" *Linguistics* 49 (June 1969): 74-91.

Harman, Gilbert. "Book Review." *Philosophical Review* April 1968, 229-34.

Kampf, Louis. "Books." *College English* 28 (1967): 403.

Prideaux, G.D. "Cartesian Linguistics." *Canadian Journal of Linguistics* Fall 1967, 50.

Salmon, Vivian. "Reviews." *Journal of Linguistics* 5 (1969): 165-87.

Spooner, Susan A. and Staff. "Summaries and Comments." *Review of Metaphysics* 20 (1967): 539.

Uitti, Karl D. "Descartes and Port-Royal In Two Diverse Retrospects." *Romance Philology* 23 (1969): 75-85.

Zimmer, Karl E. "Notes and Reviews." *International Journal of American Linguistics* 34 (1968): 290-303.

Selected Readings

Allan, Keith. "Shorter Notices." *Journal of Linguistics* 10 (1974): 217-20.

Cointelpro

Navasky, Victor S. "Cointelpro: The FBI's Secret War on Political Freedom." *New York Times Book Review* 14 March 1976.

Safire, William. "Orchestrating Outrage." *New York Times* 8 December 1975, 31.

Current Issues in Linguistic Theory

Lamb, Sydney. "Current Issues in Linguistic Theory." *American Anthropologist* 69 (1967): 411-15.

Ohmann, Richard. "The Theory of Talk." *Partisan Review,* 32 (Summer 1965): 457.

Wilks, Yorick. "Review of Chomsky: Current Issues in Linguistic Theory." *Linguistics,* no. 33 (1967): 95-101.

Essays on Form and Interpretation

Grosu, Alexander. "Essays on Form and Interpretation." *Journal of Linguistics* 15 (1979): 356-64.

Langendoen, D. Terence. "Essays on Form and Interpretation." *The Journal of Philosophy* 75 (1978): 270-79.

Leiber, Justin. "Essays on Form and Interpretation." *Review of Metaphysics* 32 (1978): 131.

For Reasons of State

Beichman, Arnold. "Noam Chomsky Turns Political Analyst." *Christian Science Monitor* 8 August 1973, 10.

"For Reasons of State." *Choice* 10 (1973): 1073.

Head, Simon. "Story Without End." *New York Review of Books,* 9 August 1973, 26.

Lehmann-Haupt, Christopher. "The Burden of Noam Chomsky." *New York Times* 2 August 1973, 33.

Steck, Henry J. "The Contemporary Scene." *Library Journal* 98 (1973): 1467.

Todd, Richard. "Left, Right, Gonzo!" *Atlantic* 232 (1973): 97.

Wolin, Sheldon S. "For Reasons of State." *New York Times Book Review,* 30 September 1973, 31.

Human Rights and American Foreign Policy

Pilgrim, C.M. "Human Rights and American Foreign Policy." *International Affairs* (London) 55 (1979): 644-5.

Language and Learning

Gruber, Howard E. "Learning Learning." *New York Times Book Review,* 19 October 1980, VII: 15.

Hacking, Ian. "Chomsky and His Critics." *New York Review of Books* 23 October 1980, 47.

Karmos, Joseph. "Language and Learning." *Phi Delta Kappan* 62 (1980): 287.

"Language and Learning: The Debate Between Jean Piaget and Noam Chomsky." *Psychology Today* December 1980, 119.

Language and Mind

Bracken, Harry M. "Chomsky's Language and Mind." *Dialogue,* September 1970, 236-47.

Hamlyn, D.W. "Language and Mind." *Metaphilosophy* 1 (1970): 268-72.

Harman, Gilbert. "Reviews." *Language* 49 (1973): 453-64.

Hulbert, Debra. "Bookmarks." *Prairie Schooner* 46 (1972-73): 370.

Langendoen, D. Terence. "Chomsky on Language." *American Speech* 45 (1970): 129-34.

Steiner, George. "The Tongues of Men." *New Yorker* 45 (1969): 217-36.

"Summaries and Comments." *Review of Metaphysics* 23 (1969): 342.

Thompson, Janna L. "Language and Mind." *Journal of the British Society for Phenomenology* 1 (1970): 61-5.

Language and Responsibility

Berman, Paul. "Language and Responsibility." *New Republic,* 18 February 1979, 39.

Davidson, Alice. "Language." *Library Journal* 15 April 1979, 951.

Hall, Robert A. Jr. "Language." *New York Times Book Review* 22 April 1979, 41.

Harman, Gilbert. "Specialist and Citizen." *Nation* 228 (1979): 345-47.

"Language and Responsibility." *Choice* 16 (1979): 516.

Quinton, Anthony. "Further Chomsky Tremors." *New Statesman* 98 (1979): 240-42.

Robinson, Paul. "Language and Responsibility." *New York Times Book Review*, 25 February 1979, 84.

Schott, Webster. "A Grammar of Conscience." *Washington Post*, 11 March 1979, F:6.

Open Secret

Chace, James. "Open Secret, The Kissinger-Nixon Doctrine in Asia." *New York Times* 10 December 1972, Sect 7, 2.

Peace in the Middle East

Avishai, Bernard. "The Jewish State in Question." *New York Review of Books* 23 January 1975, 34.

Collingwood, C. "Peace in the Middle East?" *Journal of Contemporary Asia* 5 (1975): 365-8.

Draper, Theodore. "War Between the States." *New Republic* 26 October 1974, 21-8.

Grossman, Edward. "A Modest Proposal." *Commentary* 59 (1975): 80.

Hayford, Elizabeth. "The Contemporary Scene." *Library Journal* 99 (1974): 3191.

Hoadland, Jim. "Reflections on the Middle East." *Washington Post* 29 December 1974, Books, 1.

Kelley, J.B. "In the Middle East Labyrinth." *Times Literary Supplement*, no. 3848 (1955), 1485.

Levin, N. Gordon Jr. "Noam Chomsky and Israel." *Dissent* 22 (1975): 276-86.

Longrigg, Stephen H. "Peace in the Middle East?" *Asian Affairs* 63 (1976): 198-9.

"Peace in the Middle East?" *Discussion* 171 (1974): 32-2.

Walzer, Michael. "Peace in the Middle East?: Noam Chomsky Argues an Israeli and Arab Talk." *New York Times Book Review*, 6 October 1974, 5.

Political Economy of Human Rights

Berger, Alan. "The Political Economy of Human Rights." *Politics Today* 7 (1980): 60.

Fiskin, James S. "The Political Economy of Human Rights." *New Republic*, 6 September 1980, 37.

Glass, Charles. "American Samizdat." *New Statesman* 25 April 1980, 623-4.

Greenaway, Kristine. "Political Economy of Human Rights." *Quill and Quire* 46 (1980): 37.

Langguth, A.J. "Someone Is Watching." *Nation* 16 February 1980, 181- 4.

McQuaig, Linda. "Genocide in East Timor and Other Matters." *MacLeans* 93 (1960): 37.

"The Political Economy of Human Rights." *Choice* 17 (1980): 724.

Trosan, Eloise and Michael Yates. "The Political Economy of Human Rights." *Monthly Review* 32 (1981): 43-9.

"The Washington Connection and Third World Fascism." *Humanist* 41 (1980): 44.

Problems of Knowledge and Freedom

Flew, Anthony. "Problems of Knowledge and Freedom." *Philosophy* 48 (1973): 194-5.

Gavin, Kenneth J. "Problems of Knowledge and Freedom." *Choice* 9 (1972): 378.

Gavin, Kenneth J. "What a Piece of Work Is Man!: Varied Lights on a Dark Mystery." *America* 125 (1971): 522.

Lehmann-Haupt, Christopher. "Back to Freedom and Dignity?" *New York Times* 22 December 1971, 33.

Schochet, Gordon J. "Problems of Knowledge and Freedom: The Russell Lectures." *Library Journal* 96 (1971): 3762.

Steiner, George. "Problems of Knowledge and Freedom: The Russell Lectures." *New York Times Book Review,* 9 January 1972, 25.

"The Voice of the Dove." *Times Literary Supplement* no. 3667 (1972), 359.

Reflections on Language

Andor, J. "Reviews." *Linguistics* no. 209, July 1978, 71-81.

"Battles of Mind." *Economist* 27 March 1976, 116.

Beattle, G.W. "Reflections on Reflections on Language." *Linguistic* 17 (1979): 907-23.

Cortius, H. Brandt. "Reflections on Language." *Kennis en Methode* 1 (1977): 181-9.

Davies, L.P. "Reflections.[2]." *Et Cetera* 35 (June 1978): 207-9.

Gellner, Ernest. "Reflections on Language." *Philosophy of the Social Sciences* 7 (1977): 421-4.

Harman, Gilbert. "Chomsky's Structures." *Partisan Review* 45 (1978): 463-6.

Hayman, Ronald. "Holes and Corners." *Encounter* 47 (1976): 71-6.

Hirsch, David H. "Deep Metaphors and Shallow Structures." *Sewanee Review* 85 (1977): 153-66.

Marcotte, Edward. "Disciplining the Tower of Babel." *Nation* 222 (1976): 570.

Searle, John. "The Rules of the Language Game." *Times Literary Supplement* no. 3887 (1976): 1118-20.

Shaumyan, Sebastian. "Reflections on Language." *New Republic*, 13 March 1976, 34.

Sturrock, John. "Reflections on Language." *New York Times Book Review*, 15 February 1976, VII, 3.

"This Week's Arrivals." *Christian Century* 93 (1976): 466.

Williams, Bernard. "Where Chomsky Stands." *New York Review of Books*, 11 November 1976, 43.

Rules and Representations

Hacking, Ian. "Chomsky and His Critics." *New York Review of Books* 23 October 1980, 47-50.

Richardson, Ken. "Aboard Noam's Ark." *New Statesman* 101 (1981): 18.

"Rules and Representations." *Choice* 18 (1980): 390.

"Rules and Representations." *Psychology Today* 14 (1980): 116.

"Rules and Representations." *Publishers Weekley* 217 (1980): 82.

Von Schon, Catherine. "Rules and Representations." *Library Journal* 105 (1980): 982.

Sound Pattern of English

Aronson, Ruth. "The Sound Pattern of English." *Review of Metaphysics* 22 (December 1968): 374-5.

Eghi, U. "Sound Pattern of English." *Kratylos* B and 14 Heft 1-1.

Hill, Kenneth and Larry Nessly. "The Sound Pattern of English." *Linguistics* 15 June 1973, 57-119.

Lightner, Theodore M. "A Note on McCawley's Review of 'The Sound Pattern of English.'" *International Journal of American Linguistics* 42 (1976): 79-82.

MacDonald, John W. "Book Reviews." *Harvard Educational Review* 39 (1969): 180-4.

McCawley, James D. "Notes and Reviews." *International Journal of American Linguistics* 40 (January 1974): 50-88.

"Phonetics and the Generation Gap." *Times Literary Supplement* 27 March 1969, 330.

"The Sound Pattern of English." *Choice* 5 (1969): 1442.

Studies on Semantics

Bellert, Irena. "Reviews." *Linguistics,* 125 (1974), 109-14.

Brekle, Herbert E. and Philip Luelsdorff. "Notes on Chomsky's Extended Standard Version." *Foundations of Language* 12 (January 1975):367-81.

Frank, William A. and Staff. "Summaries and Comments." *Review of Metaphysics* 27 (1974): 605-6.

Leiber, Justin. "Studies on Semantics in Generative Grammar." *Review of Metaphysics* 27 (1974): 605-6.

Peng, Fred C.C. "Studies on Semantics in Generative Grammar." *American Anthropologist* 75 (1973): 1918-20.

"Profoundly Meaningful." *Times Literary Supplement,* 7 July 1972, 773.

Sampson, G. "Studies on Semantics in Generative Grammar." *Journal of Literary Semantics* 4 (1976): 103.

Syntactic Structure

Staal, J.F. "Reviews." *Journal of Symbolic Logic* 31 (1966): 245-51.

Topics in Theory of Generative Grammar

Bellert, Irena. "Topics in the Theory of Generative Grammar." *Linguistics* 53 (October 1969): 107-17.

Matthews, Peter H. "Topics in the Theory of Generative Grammar." *Lingua* (Amsterdam) 19 (1970): 297.

"Semantic Hay." *Times Literary Supplement,* 3429 (1967): 1073.

Articles

Abel, Lionel. "The Position of Noam Chomsky." *Commentary* 47 (1969): 35-44; *Discussion* 48 (1969): 9-10.

Abel, Lionel. "Seven Heroes of the New Left." *New York Times Magazine,* 5 May 1968, VI, 30.

Anderson, Stephen R. "On the Role of Deep Structure in Semantic Interpretation." *Foundations of Language* 7 (1971): 387-96.

Atherton, Margaret. "Tacit Knowledge and Innateness." *Philosophy Forum* 3 (1972): 3-11.

Bach, Emmon. "Comments on the Paper by Chomsky." In *Formal Syntax.* Peter W. Culicover, Thomas Wascow and Adrian Akmajian, eds. New York: Academic, 1977, 133-55.

See: *On Wh-Movement* (Sect 1-2)

Barnes, Jonathan. "Mr. Locke's Darling Notion." *Philosophical Quarterly* 22 (1972): 193-214.

Bezzel, Chris. "Some Problems of a Grammar of Modern German Poetry." *Foundations of Language* 5 (1969): 470-87.

Blakeslee, Sandra. "When Children Talk, Scientists Listen." *New York Times,* 4 April 1973, 38.

Bouma, L. "Major Currents In Modern Linguistics: Chomsky and Transformational Grammar." *Modern Language Journal* (1959): 463.

Bowers, F. "The Deep Structure of Abstract Nouns." *Foundations of Language* 5 (1969): 520-33.

Bracken, Harry M. "Chomsky's Variations on a Theme by Descartes." *Journal of the History of Philosophy* 8 (1970): 180-92.

———. "Minds and Learning: The Chomskian Revolution." *Metaphilosophy* 4 (1973): 229-45.

———. "Descartes-Orwell-Chomsky: Three Philosophies of the Demonic." *Human Context* 4 (1972): 522-51.

Bruner, J.S. "From Communications to Language—A Psychological Perspective." *Cognition* 3 (1974-75): 255-87.

Bucci, Wilma. "Extended Generative Semantics: An Operational Approach." *Foundations of Language* 13 (1975): 1-23.

Butters, Ronald R. "Dialect Variants and Linguistic Deviance." *Foundations of Language* 7 (1971): 239-56.

Catania, A. Charles. "Chomsky's Formal Analysis of Natural Languages: A Behavioral Translation." *Behaviorism* 1 (1972): 1-15.

Chafe, Wallace L. "Idiolaticity As An Anomaly in the Chomskyan Paradigm." *Foundations of Language* 4 (1968): 109-27.

Clarke, Desmond M. "Innate Ideas: Descartes and Chomsky." *Philosophical Studies* 34 (1976): 52-63.

Cohen, David. "Psychologists on Psychology." *Taplinger* (1977): 72-100.

Cohen, L. Jonathan. "Applications of Inductive Logic to Theory of Language." *American Philosophical Quarterly* 7 (1970): 299-310.

Cooper, David E. "Innateness: Old and New." *Philosophical Review* 81 (1972): 465-83.

————. "The Underdetermination of Grammar." *Methodology and Science* 10 (1977): 177-88.

Cummings, Nancy Pekin. "The Relevance of Linguistic Theory to the Problem of Free Will." *Proceedings of the New Mexico, West Texas Philosophical Society* 4 (1974): 9.

Curtis, Tom. "Bourne, MacDonald, Chomsky, and the Rhetoric of Resistance." *Antioch Review* 29 (1969): 245-52.

Daly, Richard. "On Arguments Against the Empirical Adequacy of Finite State Grammar." *Philosophy of Science* 39 (1972): 461-754.

Davis, Steven. "Speech Arts, Performance and Competence." *Journal of Pragmatics* 3 (1979): 497-505.

Debray, R., J.P. Faye, J. Roubaud and M. Ronat. "Narration and Power-Massacres and Media-Discussion with Chomsky, Noam and Debray, Regis." *Change Paris* 38 (1979): 103-22.

Dieltjens, Louis. *Rule-Governed Creativity: An Analysis of the Concept in the Work of Noam Chomsky.* Inst. Voor Toege paste Linguistiek. Louvain: University Catholique, 1971.

Dougherty, Ray C. "Einstein and Chomsky on Scientific Methodology." *Linguistics* 167 (23 January 1976): 5-14.

———. "An Interpretive Theory of Phonominal Reference." *Foundations of Language* 5 (1969): 488-519.

Drach, Margaret. "The Creative Aspect of Chomsky's Use of the Notion of Creativity." *Philosophical Review* 90 (Jan 1981): 44-65.

Dresher, B. Elan and Norbert Hornstein. "On Some Supposed Contributions of Artificial Intelligence to the Scientific Study of Language." *Cognition* 4(1976): 321-98.

Dudek-Piatek, Zdzislawa. "Piaget's Constructivism and Contemporary Controversy on the Origin of Language." *Reports on Philosophy* (1978): 67-76.

Earle, William. "The Political Responsibilities of Philosophers." *Ethics* 79 (1968): 10-3.

Edger, Richard. "Chomsky Stirs French Storm in a Demitasse." *New York Times* 1 January 1981, 2.

Fellman, J. "Concerning the Validity of the Term Cartesian Linguistics." *Linguistics* 182 (1976): 35-7.

Fisher, John A. "Knowledge of Rules." *Review of Metaphysics* 28 (1974): 237-60.

Fisher, John B. "The Concept of Structure in Freud, Levi Strauss and Chomsky." *Philosophy Research Archives* 1023 (1975): 247.

Gardner, H. "Encounter at Royaumont (Piaget and Chomsky)." *Psychology Today* 13 (1979): 14-5.

Gibson, James J. "Are There Sensory Qualities of Objects?" *Synthese* 19 (1969): 408-9.

Gibson, Roger F. "Are There Really Two Quines?" *Erkenntnis* 15 (1980): 349-70.

Grandy, Richard E. "Grammatical Knowledge and States of Mind." *Behaviorism* 1 (1972): 16-21.

Haas, William. "Syntax and Semantics of Ordinary Language: Part 2." *The Aristotelian Society: Supplementary Volume* 49 (1975): 147-69.

Habermas, Jurgen. "Towards a Theory of Communicative Competence." *Inquiry* 13 (1970): 360-75.

Harman, Gilbert H. "Psychological Aspects of the Theory of Syntax." *The Journal of Philosophy* 64 (1967): 75-87.

Harnish, Robert M. "Searle on Katz's Semantic Theory." *Southwestern Journal of Philosophy* 8 (1977): 23-32.

Henderson, Connie. "Chomsky." *Gnosis* 1 (1975): 11-20.

Henderson, M.M.T. "Redundancy, Markedness, and Simultaneous Constraints in Phonology." *Language* 52 (1976): 314-25.

Hernstein, R.J. "Whatever Happened to Vaudeville: A Reply to Professor Chomsky." *Cognition* 1 (1972): 301-5.

Hintikka, Jaakko. "On the Any-Thesis and the Methodology of Linguistics." *Linguistics and Philosophy* 4 (1980): 102-22.

Hockett, Charles F. "State of the Art." In *Janua Linguarum*, Ser Minor, No. 73 1968.

Hockney, Donald. "The Bifurcation of Scientific Theories and Indeterminary of Translation." *Philosophy of Science* 42 (1975): 411-27.

Hook, Sidney. "The Political Fantasies of Noam Chomsky." *Humanist* 30 (1970): 26-9.

———. "The Knight of the Double Standard." *Humanist* 31 (1971): 29-34.

———. "The Knight Comes a Cropper." *Humanist* 31 (1971): 34-5.

Hope, Edward R. "Non-Syntactic Constraints on Lisu Noun Phrase Order." *Foundations of Language* 10 (1973): 79-109.

Horecky, J. "On the Marxist Conception of Language." *Teorie a Methoda* 7 (1975): 89-94.

Jackson, Laura (Ridling). "Supplementary Comment Concerning George Watson's Thinking on Noam Chomsky." *Denver Quarterly* 10 (1975): 19-25.

Jenkins, Lyle. "The Genetics of Language." *Linguistics and Philosophy* 3 (1979): 105-19.

Jubien, Michael. "The Intensionality of Ontological Committment." *Nous* 6 (1972): 378-87.

Kates, Carol A. "A Critique of Chomsky's Theory of Grammatical Competence." *Forum Linguisticum* 1 (1976): 15-24.

Katz, Jerrold J. "Chomsky on Meaning." *Language* 56 (1980): 1-41.

———. "Interpretative Semantics vs Generative Semantics." *Foundations of Language* 6 (1970): 220-59.

———. "Recent Issues in Semantic Theory." *Foundations of Language* 3 (1967): 124-94.

———. "The Theory of Semantic Representation." *Erkenntnis* 13 (1978): 63-109.

———. "Where Things Now Stand With the Analytic-Synthetic Distinction." *Synthese* 28 (1974): 283-319.

Kaufer, David S. "The Competence/Performance Distinction in Linguistic Theory." *Philosophy of the Social Sciences* 9 (1979): 257-75.

Keesing, Roger M. "Transformational Linguistics and Structural Anthropology." *Cultural Hermeneutics* 2 (1974): 243-66.

Kitcher, Philip. "The Nativist's Dilemma." *Philosophical Quarterly* 28 (1978): 1-16.

Kuroda, S.Y. "Anton Marty and the Transformational Theory of Grammar." *Foundations of Language* 9 (1972): 1-36.

———. "Geach and Katz on Presupposition." *Foundations of Language* 12 (1974): 177-201.

Labedz, L. "Chomsky Revisted." *Encounter* 55 (1980): 28-35.

Lacey, Hugh M. "The Scientific Study of Linguistic Behavior: A Perspective on the Skinner-Chomsky Controversy." *Journal for the Theory of Social Behavior* 4 (1974): 17-51.

———. "Psychological Conflict and Human Nature." *Journal for the Theory of Social Behavior* 10 (1980); 131-56.

Land, S.K. "Cartesian Language Test and Professor Chomsky." *Linguistics* 122 (1974): 11-24.

Lehmann-Haupt, Christopher. "More Viking Modern Masters." *New York Times,* 14 December 1970, 41.

Leiber, Justin. "Philosophical Aspects of Recent Work in Linguistics." *Philosophical Forum* (Boston) 6 (1975): 343-65.

Lepore, Ernest. "Reply to Professor Root's 'Speaker Intuitions.'" *Philosophical Studies* 32 (1977): 211-5.

Levin, Michael E. "A Definition of a Priori Knowledge." *Journal of Critical Analysis* 6 (1975): 1-8.

————. "Explanation and Prediction in Grammar (And Semantics)." *Midwest Studies in Philosophy* 2 (1977): 128-37.

Lockwood, Michael. "On Predicating Proper Names." *The Philosophical Review* 84 (1975): 471-98.

Loewenberg, Ina. "Identifying Metaphors." *Foundations of Language* 12 (1975): 315-38.

Luria, A.R. "Scientific Perspectives and Philosophical Dead Ends in Modern Linguistics." *Cognition* 3 (1974-75): 377-85.

MacIntyre, Alasdair. "Noam Chomsky's View of Language." *Listener* 79 (1968): 685-6.

Margolis, Joseph. "Mastering a Natural Language: Rationalists versus Empiricists." *Diogenes,* Winter 1973, 41-57.

Marshall, J.C. "The Adequacy of Grammars." *The Aristotelian Society: Supplementary Volume 44 (1970): 157-74.*

Matthews, Gareth B. "Movravcsik on Individuals and Their Essences." *Journal of Philosophy* 73 (1976): 598-9.

Matthews, Peter H. "The Adequacy of Grammars." *The Aristotelian Society: Supplementary Volume* 44 (1970): 175-90.

Matthews, Robert J. "Concerning a 'Linguistic Theory' of Metaphor." *Foundations of Language* 7 (1971): 413-25.

Mayher, J.S. "Introduction to Chomskyan Science." *Et Cetera* 35 (1978): 125-35.

McCawley, James D. "Concerning the Base Component of a Transformational Grammar." *Foundations of Language* 3 (1968): 243-69.

McLeish, J. and J. Martin. "Verbal Behavior: A Review and Experimental Analysis." *Journal of General Psychology* 93 (1975): 3-66.

Mehta, V. "Onward and Upward with the Arts: Linguistics." *New Yorker*, 8 May 1971, pp. 44-8.

Meisal, J.M. "On the Possibility of Non-Cartesian Linguistics." *Linguistics,* 122 (1974): 25-38.

Miel, Jan. "Pascal, Port-Royal, and Cartesian Linguistics." *Journal of the History of Ideas* 30 (1969): 261-71.

Miller, J. "A Note on So-Called 'Discovery Procedures.'" *Foundations of Language* 10 (1973): 123-39.

Miller, Robert S. "Chomsky Castigated." *New York Times* 6 September 1970, IV, 11.

Miner, Kenneth L. "English Inflectional Endings and Unordered Rules." *Foundations of Language* 12 (1975): 339-65.

Mitgang, Herbert. "Publishing: Books Due on 'Sam' and Tarnower." *New York Times* 5 December 1980, III, 29.

Includes report of telephone interview with Chomsky regarding Robert Faurisson book.

99

Moravcsik, Julius M.E. "Linguistic Theory and the Philosophy of Language." *Foundations of Language* 3 (1967): 209-33.

———. "Competence, Creativity, and Innateness." *Philosophical Forum* 1 (1969): 407-37.

———. "Subcategorization and Abstract Terms." *Foundations of Language* 6 (1970): 473-87.

———. "The Discernibility of Identicals." *Journal of Philosophy* 73 (1976): 587-98.

Newmeyer, Frederick J. "On the Alleged Boundary Between Syntax and Semantics." *Foundations of Language* 6 (1970): 178-86.

Nielsen, Kai. "Social Science and Hard Data." *Cultural Hermeneutics* 2 (1973): 115-42.

Nyiri, J.C. "No Place for Semantics." *Foundations of Language* 7 (1971): 56-69.

Oliver, G. Benjamin. "The Ontological Structure of Linguistic Theory." *The Monist* 53 (1969): 262-79.

———. "Underlying Realities of Language." *The Monist* 57 (1973): 408-29.

Olshewsky, Thomas M. "Deep Structure: Essential Transcendental or Pragmatic?" *The Monist* 57 (1973): 430-42.

———."On the Notion of a Rule." *Philosophia* 6 (1967): 267-88.

Pawlowski, Tadeusz. "Linguistics and the Semiotic Theory of Culture." *Scientia* 109 (1974): 483-7.

Putnam, Hilary. "The Innateness Hypothesis and Explanatory Models in Linguistics." *Synthese* 17 (1967): 12-22.

Rechtin, Lisbeth. "The Subject-Predicate Distinction Revisted." *Philosophical Linguistics* 4 (1972): 70-97.

Reinhold, Robert. "Five Scholars Talk About . . . Talking." *New York Times,* 10 January 1969, p. 44.

Richardson, Ken. "Aboard Noam's Ark." *New Statesman* 101 (1981): 18.

Richelle, Marc. "Formal Analysis and Functional Analysis of Verbal Behavior: Notes on the Debate Between Chomsky and Skinner." *Behaviorism* 4 (1976): 209-21.

Roeper, Thomas. "The Chomsky Experiments." *New York Review of Books,* 28 no. 6 (1981), pp. 43-44.

Root, Michael D. "How to Simulate an Innate Idea." *Philosophy Forum* 3 (1972): 12-25.

———. "Quine's Methodological Reflections." *Metaphilosophy* 5 (1974): 36-50.

———. *Speaker Intuitions. Philosophical Studies* 29 (1976): 221-33.

Rose, James H. "Principled Limitations on Productivity in Denominal Verbs." *Foundations of Language* 10 (1973): 509-62.

Rosenberg, Jay F. "What's Happening in Philosophy of Language Today—A Metaphysician's Eye View." *American Philosophical Quarterly* 9 (1972): 101-6.

Ryle, Gilbert. "Improvisation." *Mind* 85 (1976); 69-83.

Said, Edward W. "Linguistics and the Archeology of Mind." *International Philosophical Quarterly* 11 (1971): 104-34.

Samson, Geoffrey. "Against Base Co-Ordination." *Foundations of Language* 12 (1974): 117-25.

———. "An Empiricial Hypothesis About Natural Semantics." *Journal of Philosophic Logic* 5 (1976): 209-36.

———. "A Non-Nativist Account of Language Universals." *Linguistics and Philosophy* 3 (1979): 99-104.

Schlesinger, Arthur, Jr. "Schlesinger vs. Chomsky." *Commentary* 49 (1970): 14.

Schoorl, Sjef. "Pragmatic Observations on the Active-Passive Controversy." *Journal of Pragmatics* 2 (1978): 331-59.

Schuldenfrei, Richard. "Quine in Perspective." *Journal of Philosophy* 69 (1972): 5-16.

Seuren, Pieter A.N. "Autonomous Versus Semantic Syntax." *Foundations of Language* 8 (1972): 237-65.

Shaw, J.L. "Subject and Predicate." *Journal of Indian Philosophy* 4 (1976): 155-79.

Shenker, Israel. "Chomsky is Difficult to Please." *Horizon* 13 (1971): 104-9.

———. "Experts Labor to Communicate on Animal Talk." *New York Times,* 25 September 1975, 45.

———. "Former Chomsky disciples Hurl Harsh Words at the Master." *New York Times* 10 September 1972, p. 70.

Silber, John R. "Soul Politics and Political Morality." *Ethics* 79 (1968): 14-23.

Singleton, Jane. "The Explanatory Power of Chomsky's Transformational Generative Grammar." *Mind* 83 (1974): 429-31.

Sklar, Robert. "Chomsky's Revolution in Linguistics, *Nation* 9 September 1968, 213-7.

Smart, J.J.C. "The Content of Physicalism." *Philosophical Quarterly* 28 (1978): 339-41.

Sobel, Dava. "Pigeons 'Conversation' Triggers a Debate About Language." *New York Times* 19 February 1980, sect. 3, 2.

Sober, Elliott. "Language and Psychological Reality." *Linguistics and Philosophy* 3 (1980): 395-405.

Spiceland, James. "A Critique of Chomsky's Contribution to the Rationalist-Empiricist Debate." *Dianoia* 10 (1974): 1-15.

Squadrito, Kay. "Racism and Empiricism." *Behaviorism* 7 (1979): 105-15.

Stalker, Douglas F. "Some Problems With Lakoff's Natural Logic." *Foundations of Language* 10 (1973): 527-44.

Stallcup, Kenneth L. "New Growth in Linguistics Produces Clarity, Confusion and Controversy." *New York Times* 8 January 1973, 90.

Stam, James H. "Past Linguistics and Chomsky's Future." *Journal of Psycholinguistics Research* 1 (1971):195-201.

Steinberg, Danny D. "Competence, Performance and the Psychological Invalidity of Chomsky's Grammar." *Synthese* 32 (1976): 373-86.

Steiner, George. "The Tongues of Men." *New Yorker* 15 November 1969, 217-36.

Stenius, Erik. "Syntax of Symbolic Logic and Transformational Grammar." *Synthese* 26 (1973): 57-78.

Stich, Stephen P. "Between Chomskian Rationalism and Popperian Empiricism." *British Journal for the Philosophy of Science* 30 (1979): 329-47.

———. "Empiricism, Innateness, and Linguistic Universals." *Philosophical Studies* 33 (1978): 273-86.

———. "What Every Speaker Knows." *Philosophical Review* 80 (1971): 476-96.

Strawson, P.F. "Grammar and Philosophy." *Proceedings of the Aristotelian Society* 70 (1969-70): 1-20.

Struever, N.S. "Study of Language and the Study of History." *Journal of Interdisciplinary History* 4 (1974): 401-15.

Svenonius, Lars. "Three Models for the Description of Language." *Journal of Symbolic Logic* 23 (1958): 71.

Thomas, John E. "Anamnesis in New Dress." *New Scholasticism* 51 (1977): 328-49.

Toulmin, Stephen. "Brain and Language: A Commentary." *Synthese* 22 (1971): 369-95.

———. "Reply." *Synthese* 23 (1972): 487-90.

Udell, Gerald. "On First Looking into Chomsky's Halle: An Anti-Establishment Deviationist-Reactionary 206-Line Sonnet in free verse." *American Speech* 45 (1970): 91-7.

Waldner, Ilmar. "Bare Preference and Interpersonal Utility Comparisons." *Theory and Decision* 5 (1974): 313-28.

Waller, Bruce. "Chomsky, Wittgenstein, and the Behaviorist Perspective on Language." *Behaviorism* 5 (1977): 43-59.

Warmbrod, Ken. "Philosophy and Empiricial Linguistics." *Metaphilosophy* 41 (1973); 205-28.

Wasow, Thomas. "The Innateness Hypothesis and Grammatical Relations." *Synthese* 26 (1973): 38-52.

Watson, G. "Chomsky: what has it to do with Literature?" *Times Literary Supplement* 3806 (1975), 164-5.

Wehrwein, Austin c. "A 'New English' Gaining Ground: Fresh Approach to Grammar." *New York Times* 29 December 1965, 31.

Wheatley, Jon. "Philosophy and Linguistics." *Dialogue* 5 (1967): 609-21.

Wilks, Yorick. "Decidability and Natural Language." *Mind* 80 (1971): 497-521.

————. "One Small Head Models and Theories in Linguistics." *Foundations of Language* 11 (1974): 77-95.

Williams, Bernard. "Where Chomsky Stands." *New York Review of Books* 11 November 1976, 43.

Wilson, Fred F. "Maras on Sellars on Thought and Language." *Philosophical Studies* 28 (1975): 91-102.

Yallop, Colin. "The Lord is My Goatherd: I Don't Want Him." *Interchange* (1974): 214-20.

————. "The Problem of Linguistic Universals." *Philosophia Reformata* 43 (1978): 61-72.

Yergin, Daniel. "The Chomskyan Revolution." *New York Times* 3 December 1972, VI, 42.

Yu, Paul. "Grammar and Understanding." *Canadian Journal of Philosophy* 9 (1979): 261-81.

Ziff, Paul. "The Number of English Sentences." *Foundations of Language* 11 (1974): 519-32.

Miscellaneous in English

Lichenstein, Nelson, ed. "Noam Chomsky." In *Political Profiles: The Johnson Years.* New York: Facts on file 4 (1976): 104-5.

Moritz, Charles, ed. "Chomsky, (Avram) Noam." In *Yearbook 1970.* New York: H.W. Wilson, 1970, 1971. pp. 80-3.

Schoenebaum, Eleanora, ed. "Noam Chomsky." In *Political Profiles: The Nixon/Ford Years.* New York: Facts on File 5 (1979); 125.

Foreign Publications

Books

Báez, San José Valerio. *Introducción crítica a la gramática generativa.* Barcelona: Planeta, 1975. 341 p.

Collinder, Björn. *Noam Chomsky und die Generative Grammatik: Eime Kritische Betrachtung.* Uppsala: Almquul & Wilksells, 1970. 29 p. (Acte Societalis Linguuticae Upsaliensis, Nova Series 2:1).

Searle, John R. *La revolución de Chomsky en lingüística.* Trans. Carlos Manzano. Barcelona: Editorial Anagrama, 1973, 71 p.

Book Reviews

Bymann, W. "Cartesianische Linguistik." *kratylos* (Wiesbaden), Band 16 HEFT 2-122.

Gottschalk, K.D. "Chomsky: Selected Readings." *Die Neueren Sprachen* (Frankfurt Am Main), June 1974, p. 273.

Nickel, G. "Aspects of the Theory of Syntax." *Archiv Für Das Studium Der Neueren Sprachen und Literaturen* (Braumschweig, Germany) BAND 208 HEFT 3-206.

Tellier, A.R. "Chomsky: Selected Readings." *Etudes Anglaises* (Paris) 27 (1974): 350.

Viereck, W. "Cartesian Linguistics." *Die Neueren Sprachen* (Frankfurt Am Main), August 1972, p. 490.

Articles

Artal, A. Garcia. "Chomsky (1957): Pardigma o preparadigma?" *Teorema* 5 (1975): 285-93.

Bense, Elisabeth. "Mentalismus in der Sprach-Theoric Noam Chomsky." (Skripten Linguistik und Kommunikationwissenschaft, 2) *Scriptor Verlag* (1973): 111-17.

Berger, H. "Van De Saussure Tot Chomsky." *Tijdscher. Filosof.* 32 (1970); 175-96.

Carrillo, Victor L. "Las tres lingüísticas." *Revista Venezolana de Filosofia* (1976): 53-84.

Enthoven, Jean-Paul. "Genocide: Chomsky ne Savait Pas." *Nouvel Observateur* 28 December 1980, 30.

Gardner, Howard. "Piaget et Chomsky s'affrontent." *Psychologie* 118, Nov. 1979, 44-6.

Guiliani, M.V. "L'Analisi Formale del Linguaggio." *Pensiero E Linguaggio In Operazioni* 1 (1970): 228-31.

Havet, J. and others. "Le Tendenze Della Ricerca Filosofica Contemporanea." *Filosofia* 21 (1970): 461-508.

Hierro, José. "Conocimiento, creencia y competencia lingüística." *Teorema Mono* 1 (1974): 81-98.

Hubien, Hubert. "Philosophie Analytique et Linguistique Moderne." " *Dialectica* 22 (1968): 96-119.

Jacob, Andre. "L'Analyse Formelle des Langues Naturelles." *Les Etudes Philosophiques* 24 (1969): 396-99.

Kaufmann, J.N. "Psychologie de la 'Consciencé et Science du 'Behavior'." *Philosophiques* 4 (1977): 313-26.

Kung, Guido. "Expérience Spontanée Et Theorie Rationnelle." *Studies in Philosophy* 36 (1976): 90-106.

Largeault, J. "Dialogues avec Mitsou Ronat." *Archives de Philosophie* 41 (1978): 693-6.

Markis, Dimitrios K. "Bedeutung und Übersetzung: Quine Und Das Problem Der Übersetzungstheorie (in Greek). *Philosophia* (Athens) 4 (1974): 77-119.

Mayr, Franz K. Philosophische Implikatignen Amerikanischer Linguistic: Noam Chomsky. *Zeitschrift fur Philosophische forschung* 27 (1973): 407-29.

Mourelos, G. La Notion de Structure Dans La Philosophie Moderne (in Greek) *Annales D'Esthetique* 9-10 (1970-71): 126-44.

Ninet, Antonio Garcia. "Del Innatismo de Katz y Chomsky al constructivismo del Piaget." *Dialogos* 8 (1972); 69-83.

also in: *Estudios Filosoficos* 22 (1973): 249-60.

Oleron, Pierre. "Le Behaviorisme en Question." *Revue Philosophique de la France et de l'Etranger* 96 (1971): 417-34.

Panaccio, Claude. "L'explication en Grammaire Transformationnelle." *Dialogue* (Canada) 18 (1979): 307-41.

Parret, Herman. "Indépendance Et Interdépendance Da La Forme Et De La Fonction Du Langage." *Revue Philosophique de Louvain* 73 (1975): 56-78.

Pochtar, Ricardo. "El examen de ingenios y la lingüística cartesiana." *Revista Latinoamericana de Filosofia* 2 (1976): 179-86.

Ponzio, Augusto. "Grammatica generativa fenomenologica." *Filosofia* 22 (1971): 77-96.

Quesada, J. Daniel. "El programa psicolingüístico de Chomsky: Una evaluación." *Teorema* 5 (1975): 469-86.

―――. "Las implicaciones epistemologicas de la hipotesis chomskyana de las ideas innnatas." *Teorema* 3 (1973): 265-87.

Roca, Ignacio M. "Lingüística, filosofía y psicologia en el pensamiento de Noam Chomsky." *Convivium* 42 (1974): 29-50.

Rothschild, Thomas. "Linguistik In Der Schule." *Sprache im Technischen Zeitalter* 9 (1970): 34-44.

Roy, Claude. "Le gauchisme, maladie sénile du communisme?" *Le Nouvel Observateur* no. 815, 21 juin 1980, 56-60.

Schleifer, M. "Behaviorisme et Psychologie." *Philosophiques* 4 (1977): 327-34.

Soares gomes, Francisco. "Estruturalismo: Da interioridade ao saber." *Revista Portuguesa de Filosofia* 32 (1976): 143-70.

Spolsky, Bernard. "Programmiertes Lehren Von Fremdsprachen." *Sprache im Technischen Zeitalter* 9 (1970): 1-10.

Szabo, Istvan. "Philosophy of Language and the Generative Theory of Language." (in Hungarian) *Magyar Filozofiai Szemle* 4 (1980): 552-67.

Thibaud, Paul. "Le Camabodge, Les Droits De L'Homme Et L'Opinion Inter-nationale." *Esprit* September 1980. pp. 112-23.

Vidal-Nauquet, Pierre. "De Faurisson et de Chomsky." in Les Juifs (book) *La mémoire et le présent*. F. Maspero(?), 1981 (?).

———. "Un Eichmann de Papier: Vivre avec Faurisson?" *Esprit* September 1980 pp. 50-52.

Voss, Josef. "Noam Chomsky et La Linguistique Cartesienne." *Revue Philosophique de Louvain* 71 (1973): 512-38.

Weydt, Harald. Noam Chomsky's Werk; Kritik, Kommentar, bibliographie. (Tübinger Beiträge zur Linguistik, 70) TBL Verlag Narr, 1976, pp. 78-102.

Xirua, Ramón. "Innatismo de ideas y de no-ideas." *Dianoia* 18 (1972); 138-51.

Fodor, Jerry, on "language of thought," 4

Freud, Sigmund, on accessibility of mental representations, 23

Gall, Franz Josef, on organology, 3

Generative grammar, 25-26; as a part of Biology, 29

Gleitman, Lila, work on language acquisition in blind children, 48

Grammar: as rules of the mind, 13; postulation of, 13-14; generative, 25-26, 29; traditional, 25, 27, 28; represents state of the organism, 26; as characteristics of peoples, 29; universal, 30, 36-37; steady state in, 36; evolution and, 37; transformational, 38

Hale, Kenneth, work on Walbiri, 45

Hume, David, and accessibility of ideas, 23

Initial state of human mind, 30, 36, 49; common to the species, 49

Intelligence: human as specific biological system, 2, 7; artificial, 16

Jerison, Harry, speculation about origins of language, 40

Jespersen, Otto, grammarian, 28

Kant, Immanuel, on mental principles, 20

Knowledge: as practical ability, 11; systems of attaining, 19; as true belief questioned, 21; as consequences of systems of principles, 21-22.

LaForge, Louis, expositor of René Descartes, 5; on difference between men and machines, 5

Language: Descartes on, 6, 7; creative aspects of, 6, 7; internal modularity of, 17-18; as a political notion, 29-30; research on framework of, 31; disparity between input and output, 31; parameters of, 35, 45; principles of 35; system of similar to number system, 39; purity of questioned, 40; and dialect, 41; as set of behaviors, 42; computational aspect of, 43; pragmatic aspect of, 43; acquisition of by blind children, 48; child acquisition of, 47

Linguistics: research in, 25-50; as a natural science, 27, 35-36

Machines, distinction between men and, 5

Marshall, John, and "new organology," 3

Mechanics, 5-7; of Descartes, 5, 6; of Newton, 5

Mental organs, 3, 4, 7, 22

Mental representations, 1, 2, 3, 4, 9, 10, 17; format of, 3; rule problem of, 3; causal role of, 4, 17; accessibility of, 4, 23; ontological status, 4; Cartesian postulation of, 9; nature of, 13-14; binding principle of, 13, 24; rigidity principle of, 14, 24; and experience, 18; Hume, Kant, and Freud on, 23; perception of crucial, 24

Metaphysics and mind, 6

Mind: viewed by Descartes as a thinking substance, 6; undifferentiated, 7; homogeneity principle regarding, 15-16, challenged, 16; Cartesian view of, 15; modular structure of, 16; binding and rigidity as innate principles of, 20; research on system of principles of, 33-34; principles of similar to biological speciation, 34

Modularity, 3, 16; Cartesian view, 15; Piagetian type of, 15; of biological systems, 16; internal aspect of language, 17

Multilingualism, 40, 41

New organology, 3, 17

Newton, Isaac, challenged Cartesian mechanics, 7-8

Number faculty: innate in humans, lacking in chimpanzees, 18; similar to language systems, 39

Plato and poverty of stimulus, 19

Poverty of stimulus, 19, 32

Predictability of behavior, 17

Premack, David, work on chimpanzee learning ability, 38

Psychology, field of discussed, 20, 46

Research, 25-50; strategies of, 44-45, 46; on internal systems, 44; computers and, 44; on language acquisition, 46-48; on individual differences, 50; on language in schizophrenia, 50

Rigidity principle in language, 16, 19, 24

Rules of the mind, 13

Schizophrenia and language, 50

Skinner, B.F., and mental systems, 10

Soul, 5, 6

Speech communities: existence of questioned, 40

Steady state: of language, 30; of human mind, 36

Transformational grammar, 38

Visual processing, 13; "rigidity principle" of, 15

Visual perception, 1